IESE CITIES IN MOTION:
INTERNATIONAL URBAN BEST PRACTICES

CITIES AND
SOCIAL COHESION:
DESIGNING MORE INCLUSIVE
URBAN AREAS

VOLUME 4

PROF. PASCUAL BERRONE
PROF. JOAN ENRIC RICART COSTA
ANA ISABEL DUCH T-FIGUERAS

IESE Business School
University of Navarra

IESE
Cities in
Motion

Preface to the Book Series

"IESE CITIES IN MOTION:
International urban best practices"

The world is experiencing the largest increase in urban growth in history. Today, more than half of the world's population lives in cities and it is forecast that the percentage of urban residents in the global population will increase to almost 70% by 2050. This unprecedented growth in urbanization has the potential to bring significant benefits for citizens, such as new jobs and well-being, along with overall economic growth. However, rapid urbanization also multiplies the number, size and complexity of the challenges faced by cities, such as increasing pressure on scarce resources, greater demand for basic infrastructure and public services, as well as greater socioeconomic inequality.

Cities must be able to solve economic, social and environmental problems simultaneously, in all cases with the aim of improving the welfare and quality of life of their residents. In their search for sustainable, equitable, connected and innovative city models, municipal leaders around the world look at the experiences of other cities to get ideas and study best practices. Although there is no "one size fits all" solution, this book series aims to help city managers in their endeavors to create urban areas that are environmentally, economically and socially sustainable. With this objective, this series will examine some of the actions, projects and initiatives that have had the best results in cities internationally, so that other cities around the world can build on the most successful approaches and adapt them to their local realities and needs.

The book series is structured on the basis of the IESE Cities in Motion model, which includes an innovative approach to the governance of cities and a new urban model for the 21st century based on 10 key areas or dimensions: human capital, social cohesion, the economy, public management, governance, mobility and transportation, the environment, urban planning, technology and international outreach. Each volume in this series provides an overview of the main challenges regarding a specific dimension and describes some of the most successful initiatives and actions that have been adopted in regard to that area in different cities around the world. Despite the fact that each area is covered in a separate volume of its own, all the key areas must be seen as different parts of a system that works as one. All the dimensions are interconnected and actions in one area affect other areas at the same time. Therefore, the available resources must be shared and managed together in order to achieve sustainable, lively, healthy and safe cities.

With this book series, we aim to contribute to the debate on smart urban governance by developing valuable ideas and innovative tools that can lead to smarter and more sustainable cities, while promoting real change at the local level and improving people's quality of life. We believe that current urban challenges are not only problems to be solved, but opportunities to be exploited.

Prior volumes of this series:

Vol. 1: *Cities and the Environment: The challenge of becoming green and sustainable,* CreateSpace, 2016.

See, **"Greening Up in the City"**. Available at: http://www.amazon.com/dp/1523965789.

"Responsible for the vast majority of the world's energy use and greenhouse gas emissions, urban areas are also the main contributors to air, noise, water and land pollution. Moreover, cities generate large quantities of waste, are voracious consumers of natural resources, and they are particularly vulnerable to natural disasters and climate change. Given the current rates of urbanization, the environmental impacts of cities are of urgent concern. This first volume of the series focuses on the effects of urbanization on our planet, analyzing the main environmental challenges that city governments face, and offering a catalog of international urban best practices on environmental issues."

Vol. 2: *Cities and Mobility & Transportation: Towards the next generation of urban mobility,* CreateSpace, 2016.

See, **"Setting the Wheels in Motion for Sustainable Transportation"**. Available at: https://www.amazon.com/dp/1533358141.

"As cities grow, the demand for mobility escalates. This stresses existing urban transport systems and infrastructures, exacerbates widespread traffic, and increases road accidents and fatalities. It also increases greenhouse gas emissions and air and noise pollution, causing serious health concerns and grave environmental repercussions. Thus, ensuring a sustainable and efficient distribution of people, goods and services is essential to cities' social and economic development. This second volume of the series focuses on the main urban mobility and transportation trends and challenges, and compiles a catalog of international best practices on sustainable urban mobility."

Vol. 3: *Cities and the Economy: Fueling growth, jobs and innovation,* CreateSpace, 2017.

See, **"Boosting Sustainable Growth via the World's Cities"**. Available at: https://www.amazon.com/dp/1535320818.

"The ability of cities to generate income, employment and well-being for its inhabitants is one of the main drivers behind today's high urbanization rates. As centers of production, innovation, creativity, trade and connectivity, urban areas are taking a leading role in stimulating global economic growth. However, cities can also be places where challenges such as inequality, unemployment, segregation and poverty, are concentrated and exacerbated. This third volume of the series reviews the trends and challenges of economic development in urban areas and debates what city governments can do to foster sustainable urban economic development. In addition, it also highlights international urban best practices fostering economic development and discusses a few notable successful initiatives."

Contents

1. Introduction

Cities have always attracted flows of diverse people. But rapid urbanization and globalization are accelerating this process, resulting in urban areas that are more diverse than ever before – economically, socially, culturally, ethnically, religiously, and in terms of people's identities and lifestyles. This new reality of highly diversified cities can be a source of new opportunities and socio-economic development for individual citizens, communities and the economy as a whole. However, it can also create important social and economic tensions. In fact, cities are places where social problems are concentrated and intensified: in urban areas we find some of the most fragmented societies, with increasing inequality, poverty, segregation, exclusion and social polarization among citizens.

Social fragmentation, inequality and segregation are among the negative consequences of rapid urbanization. The main challenge for city governments around the world is to be able **to integrate heterogeneous groups of citizens in the urban life, minimize problems of urban segregation, and use social, economic and physical diversity as a force of creativity, innovation, economic development, inclusiveness and well-being**.

In order to achieve socially cohesive societies with equal opportunities for social mobility for all, city leaders need to stimulate the positive aspects of urban diversity, while countering the negative ones. If socio-economic, cultural and ethnic diversity in cities is well managed, it can boost social cohesion, social mobility, economic development, and provide higher living standards and well-being for citizens. To accomplish this, **people must be put back at the center of local policies**. Local leaders must make a political commitment to develop urban areas that are inclusive and sustainable, where collective benefits are the priority.

Recognizing this and due to an increasing global concern for inclusive cities, in 2015 the United Nations adopted the city-specific Sustainable Development Goal, SDG 11: "Sustainable Cities and Communities: Make cities and human settlements inclusive, safe, resilient and sustainable" by 2030. Although successful integration and social cohesion in cities are very much dependent on national policies and regulations, **cities have a key role to play in achieving the goal of leaving no one behind**.

There is an urgent need for urban managers to establish frameworks and implement strategies, policies and tools that can transform urban areas into inclusive places for all. In this volume, we will assess how different local governments try to combat poverty, inequalities and problems of social exclusion in cities. We will analyze various initiatives, policies and strategies regarding social cohesion at the city level that are working well, as inspiration for other cities. Many of these initiatives and programs are cross-dimensional and directly related to other dimensions of city governance and urban management in our model. For instance, aspects of unemployment and labor inequalities are related to the *Economy*; issues of adequate housing and basic urban infrastructures to *Urban Planning*; matters of equal and fair consultation, dialogue and participation are directly related to *Governance and Civic Participation*; or aspects of access to education, culture and heritage to *Human Capital*. Therefore, policy makers and urban leaders must take a holistic approach when defining social cohesion policies and initiatives.

This book volume looks at some of the issues of social cohesion and inclusion in cities and provides some examples and ideas for finding common solutions to shared challenges in cities around the world. Following this introduction, Section 2 discusses some of the trends and major challenges regarding urban poverty, inequality and social exclusion in cities. Section 3 highlights a few successful actions and initiatives that city governments around the world have taken or are taking in order to reduce urban inequalities through urban design, infrastructure and policy. The last section of the book offers some concluding thoughts.

***

2. Trends and Challenges for Social Cohesion in Cities

Trends and challenges linked with social cohesion and inclusion are more intense and visible in cities than in any other locale. Rapid urbanization, together with other dynamics of social and demographic change, has resulted in urban areas with very heterogeneous populations in terms of economic levels, socio-cultural profiles, household composition, etc. These diverse socio-demographic profiles in cities has often given rise to a concentration of inequalities, poverty, isolated communities and informal settlements, social polarization and crime. **The main challenge for city leaders is to ensure that urban areas provide safe and healthy environments to live in, sustainable and productive economies, and social benefits to a diverse group of people.**

Social cohesion is a multi-faced transversal concept with different dimensions and a wide range of definitions.[1] Regardless of the definition used, a "cohesive society" is one that aims for "the well-being of all

---

[1] One of the first definitions of social cohesion was the one made by sociologist Emilie Durkheim in the late 19th century, focusing on "social solidarity" among different members of a group. More recently, Kearns and Forrest (2000) define social cohesion along five elements: common values and a civic culture; social order and social control; social solidarity and reductions in wealth disparities; social networks and social capital; and place attachment and identity. In another definition by UNECE (2006), social cohesion is defined as "the process of developing a community of shared values, shared challenges and equal opportunity, based on a sense of trust, hope and reciprocity among the population." Other definitions focus more on economic interests, class, state, society and status, among other factors.

its members" and includes the central notions of "inclusion", "equal opportunities", "equal rights", "integrity", "trust", "group identification", "sense of belonging" and/or "social capital". Social cohesion aggregate several aspects of people's well-being, such as economy, socio-cultural domains, demographic characteristics, education, health, security and safety, and/or job opportunities and jobs conditions. (See Figure 1.)

Figure 1. Dimensions of inclusive cities

Economic Inclusion | Social Inclusion | Inclusive Access to Services | Spatial Inclusion | Security and Safety

Source: Prepared by the authors.

The different dimensions of inclusion and social cohesion in cities are all intertwined and directly reinforce each other. For example, living in a slum does not only imply spatial exclusion, it also means being economically excluded (i.e. economic and employment opportunities in deprived neighborhoods are fewer than in the rest of the city); socially excluded (i.e. poor neighborhoods often have high concentrations of minorities); with difficulties to access certain key services and infrastructures (e.g. health, education, transport, information and communication technologies (ICTs), etc.); and where security and safety are usually not as good as in other parts of the city. Therefore, all aspects and dimensions of inclusion and exclusion in cities must be tackled in a coordinated and holistic way.

This section is going to examine some of the current challenges and trends in urban areas regarding social cohesion, such as inequalities, poverty, inadequate housing, spatial segregation, lack of access to key services and infrastructures, security, or social groups at a higher risk of social exclusion. Understanding the challenges that cities are facing and will most likely face in the years to come in terms of social cohesion and inclusion is key because social cohesion is one of the pillars of a good quality urban system.

***

2.1 Urban Poverty and Rising Income Inequalities

At the global level, remarkable progress has been made over the past decades in terms of poverty reduction, economic growth and increases in average living standards. **The number of people living in extreme poverty worldwide dropped to under 10% of the population in 2015, down from 37% in 1990** and 44% in 1981 (World Bank, 2016a).[2] However, rapid urbanization has brought about growing income disparities, various forms of inequality, deepening poverty and a higher number of people at risk of social exclusion in cities across the world.

In fact, **for the urban context, the gap between the urban rich and the urban poor has never been so wide**, with 75% of the world's cities having higher levels of income inequalities than 20 years ago (UN-Habitat, 2016b). The most unequal cities in terms of income inequality are found in emerging and developing countries. But rising urban inequality is not limited to the developing world. High levels of income inequality can also be found in cities in industrialized countries, as shown by the GINI Index,[3] which despite its limitations is the most commonly used standard measure of income inequality. (See Table 1 and Figure 2.)

---

[2] The World Bank defines "extreme poverty" as living on less than $1.90 per person per day.

[3] The GINI Index or GINI Coefficient ranges from "zero", which represents perfect equality, to "one", expressing maximal inequality (or from 0 to 100).

Table 1. Top unequal cities in the world, GINI Index, 2016

#	City (Country)	GINI Index 2016
1	Santo Domingo (Dominican Republic)	66.5
2	Nairobi (Kenya)	64.5
3	Lagos (Nigeria)	64.4
4	Johannesburg (South Africa)	63.2
5	Cape Town (South Africa)	59.2
6	Rio de Janeiro (Brazil)	55.9
7	São Paulo (Brazil)	54.9
8	Salvador (Brazil)	54.3
9	Miami (USA)	50.7
10	Houston (USA)	50.5
11	Los Angeles (USA)	50.1
12	San Jose (Costa Rica)	50.0
13	Jerusalem (Israel)	49.7
14	Kuala Lumpur (Malaysia)	49.6
15	New York (USA)	49.5

Source: Euromonitor International from national statistics (2017).

Figure 2: City population and inequality, 2016

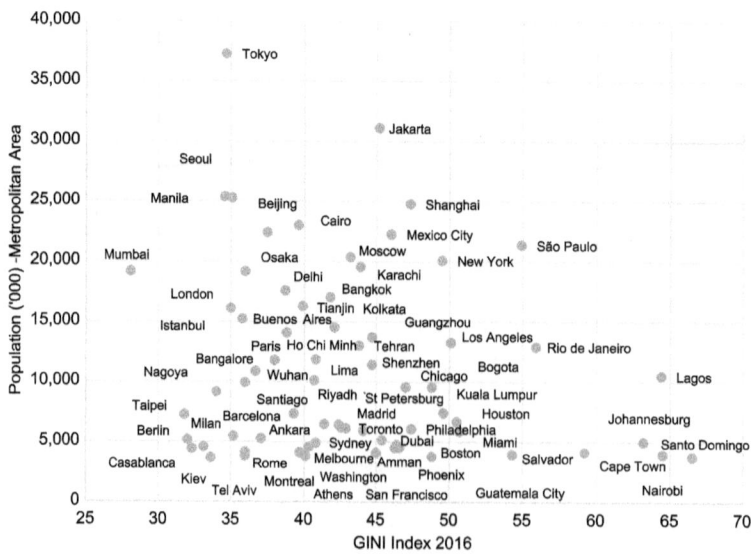

Source: Own elaboration with data from Euromonitor International (2017).

Income inequality and urban poverty can affect people's quality of life in many different ways and are two of the most severe challenges of urbanization. First, they can destabilize social cohesion, by generating social and political unrest. The social exclusion of the urban poor is evident and very prominent in their day-to-day life; and high levels of inequality can impact the levels of trust and solidarity in a society. Second, high levels of inequality can have a significant impact on the overall city's economic performance, jeopardizing economic development and economic growth. And lastly, because they also have important environmental effects - with less safe water and energy - and political repercussions - with people excluded from participating in political life, especially in cities where institutional mechanisms are weak.

Figure 3: Urban prosperity (CPI), inequality (GINI) and poverty (MPI) in selected cities

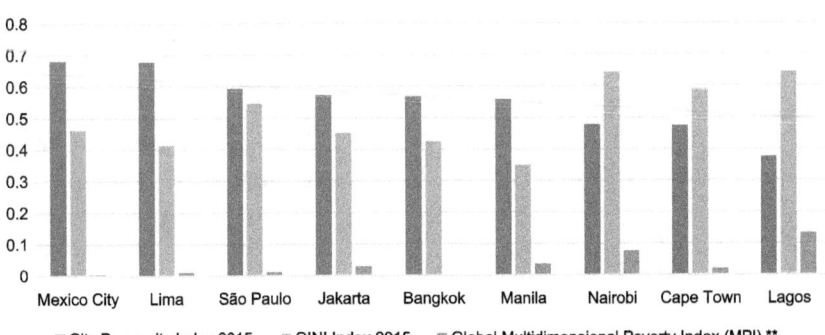

Source: Own elaboration from different sources: CPI from UN-Habitat City Prosperity Initiative (2016), GINI from Euromonitor (2017) and MPI from Global Multidimensional Poverty Index Databank (2016).

Note 1: The City Prosperity Index (CPI) is a multidimensional index based on six dimensions: productivity, infrastructure, quality of life, equity, sustainability and governance.

Note 2: The MPI measures three dimensions of poverty (Health, Education and Living Standards) using 10 different indicators.

Note 3: ** Different years from 2012 to 2014, depending on availability. When MPI at the city level was not available, the Urban MPI value for the country was used.

However, poverty and inequality refer to more than just money or income. **Both poverty and inequality are multidimensional concepts covering wider aspects and dimensions beyond money-based indicators**. Some of them will be covered in the following points, including limited access to employment opportunities (as follows) and/or to key services; lack of adequate housing and basic facilities; deficits in security and safety; among others. These dimensions of poverty and inequality are all as important as earnings and money so as to improve people's wellbeing, reduce concentration of inequalities and enhance social inclusion in urban areas. **City leaders should address issues of poverty and inequality as top priorities when defining social cohesion strategies and policies in urban areas.**

Labor inequalities

Inequalities in labor markets and labor market barriers are also important issues affecting the different dimensions of poverty and inequality. Although concerns of unemployment and labor market inequalities have been mentioned in the previous book volume, *Cities and the Economy* (Berrone, Ricart, and Duch T-Figueras, 2017), it is important to also mention them here because constraints to employment opportunities, high levels of unemployment and informal employment have important negative financial and social effects on personal life and are associated with increases in the probability of being at risk of social exclusion and poverty.

Achieving fair and equal access to labor markets in cities should be a key priority for local governments, since **well-functioning labor markets are often related with reduced poverty and inequality**. Labor-market regulations and legislation that tackle barriers to access jobs opportunities, unemployment and informal employment should be central in any city plan, since they comprise the first steps to solve income inequalities. Some of the possible policy interventions to address informality and unemployment were discussed in the previous volume, such as giving targeted support to Small and Medium Enterprises (SMEs) and providing training and education, among other initiatives. In order to foster integration and avoid segregation in cities, local managers should establish policies that ensure access to jobs and services for residents with all types of backgrounds, skills and educational levels. **Only by reducing labor inequalities and unemployment is it possible to reduce poverty and exclusion**.

***

2.2 Spatial Inequalities and Spatial Segregation

Spatial inequalities exist in a variety of forms, between rural and urban areas, small and big cities, land-locked and coastal areas, etc. Within a given city, the most visible form of spatial inequality or spatial stratification exists among neighborhoods or areas of the city. Many urban areas are often divided between wealthy and deprived zones, with clearly separated rich and poor neighborhoods. Factors such as ethnicity, culture, religion or race can also be a source of spatial stratification. For instance, Romani communities in Europe or African Americans in the USA tend to be aggregated in suburbs or specific neighborhoods.

When the population of a city is physically segregated based on particular characteristics (income level, socio-cultural status, ethnicity, etc.), problems and challenges to social cohesion become evident and create what is known as **"spatial segregation."** City dwellers who are spatially segregated in deprived areas or ethnically divided districts often cannot access other parts of the city, and see their opportunities for social and/or spatial mobility as limited.

In fact, the spatial distribution of a city is very much related to the access - or lack of access - to housing, public spaces and services, education, health, jobs, consumption, mobility and transportation, and infrastructures. It also includes exclusion from technological innovations, new optical fiber networks and internet access. Geographical separation into wealthy and poor neighborhoods thus leads to unequal public service provision and accessibility, and contributes to self-perpetuating patterns of inequality and poverty. Therefore, reducing spatial segregation is a critical factor for cities that want to achieve socially diverse communities and avoid exclusion in neighborhoods.

Issues of spatial development and spatial segregation lie at the crossroads between urban planning and social inclusion. Spatial segregation is the result of urban planning and urban shape,[4] but it is also an effect of social polarization and increasing inequalities in cities. In this volume, we will look at a few of the social aspects of spatial development in cities, and Section 3 will describe some examples of how city governments can influence city shape in a way that facilitates integration.

Slum next to a wealthy area in Mumbai, India

Source: Pixabay, CC0

---

[4] We will also look at this issue in the volume *Cities and Urban Planning*.

BOX 1: Gated Communities – The Case of Nordelta in Greater Buenos Aires, Argentina

Sometimes high-income city residents segregate themselves from other members of the city for prestige or security reasons. **Gated communities** are an example of this. They are a form of residential community that is strictly controlled, often with a closed perimeter with fences or walls, where high-income citizens create a kind of fortress for themselves.

In Argentina, these gated communities are known as "countries." Countries appeared in the 1970s, mainly as leisure spaces not far from Buenos Aires, primarily intended for weekend getaways. Over the years, what once were second homes for weekends or holidays have become home to many high-income families fleeing insecurity in the city. Nordelta, situated some 40 km. from the city of Buenos Aires, is one of the richest and best-known gated communities in the metropolitan area of Buenos Aires and one of the many examples of housing zones in expansion in Argentina: neighborhoods with 24h surveillance and private security inhabited by families looking to run away from the city's violence and insecurity feeling.

The crime index in Buenos Aires in 2016 was of 62.20, a relatively high overall level of crime (Numbeo, 2017). This feeling of insecurity and high levels of criminal activity and violence in Buenos Aires is prompting upper-class citizens to socially segregate and exclude themselves in gated communities. Today, some 45,000 people live in Nordelta, the biggest gated community in the country. It has five schools, a hospital, restaurants, a shopping mall, a hotel and a large lake for sailing.

Affordable Housing for All

Providing **adequate shelter and municipal basic services** for the rising number of urban dwellers is one of the most important challenges in cities around the world. Access to improved and affordable housing is a basic condition that determine quality of life and well-being. Improved housing is not only critical for people living in inadequate conditions, it is also key to reducing socio-economic inequalities, provides benefits for businesses that operate in cities, enhances sustainable development, attracts talent and innovation, and can even help mitigate climate change. Therefore, making proper housing more affordable to all should be a top priority for city leaders.

As more and more people move to urban areas, housing markets in cities are increasingly impacted. Today, real estate prices are rising in many cities across the globe, making it more difficult for low-income and marginalized urban dwellers to find affordable housing. The shortage in the supply of affordable housing is especially severe in developing and emerging countries, as reflected in the unprecedented proliferation of slums, to be discussed later. But this trend is also affecting cities in developed countries, triggering gentrification, which we will also address.

Local authorities can adopt different approaches when seeking to make housing more affordable and addressing related challenges. These include involving the public directly in housing development, establishing land and housing regulations, favoring mixed ownership models, coordinating land use with transportation planning policies, or rents controls, among many others. Every city requires distinct strategies and approaches, but addressing housing challenges is essential for achieving social cohesion and overcoming problems of poverty and inequality.

Table 2. Price of property as percentage of income 2016, top 10 cities

Rank	City, Country	Price of Property to Income Ratio
1	Hong Kong, Hong Kong	37.57
2	Hanoi, Vietnam	35.58
3	Mumbai, India	35.25
4	London, UK	33.51
5	Beijing, China	33.45
6	Lviv, Ukraine	32.36
7	Ho Chi Minh City, Vietnam	31.69
8	Shanghai, China	30.23
9	Shenzhen, China	30.03
10	Kiev, Ukraine	26.48

Source: Numbeo (2016).

Note: Price of Property to Income Ratio refers to apartment purchase affordability (lower is better). It is generally calculated as the ratio of median apartment prices to median familial disposable income.

Slums and Informal Settlements

Slums or informal settlements are one of the most-well known consequences of the lack of affordable housing and urban poverty. According to the United Nations, the five main defining characteristics of a slum are: (i) inadequate access to safe water; (ii) inadequate access to sanitation and infrastructure; (iii) poor housing; (iv) overcrowding; and (v) insecurity (UN-Habitat, 2016a).

Today, approximately **a quarter of the world's urban population lives in slums**. For the developing world, this figure rises to around a third of the urban population living in slums in 2014, with some countries in Sub-Saharan Africa reaching above 80% of urban residents (United Nations Statistics Division, 2016). This is a clear byproduct of rapid, unplanned urbanization. Despite the fact that the percentage of people living in informal settlements has decreased in past decades (see Figure 4), the absolute number of slum dwellers has increased – as a result of the increasing number of people moving to cities, especially in developing countries. UN-Habitat (2016b) estimates that **the number of people living in the slums of the world's developing regions reached over 880 million in 2014**, up from 791 million in 2000 and 689 million in 1990.

Figure 4: Proportion of urban population living in slums, informal settlements or inadequate housing, 1990, 2000 and 2014 (%)

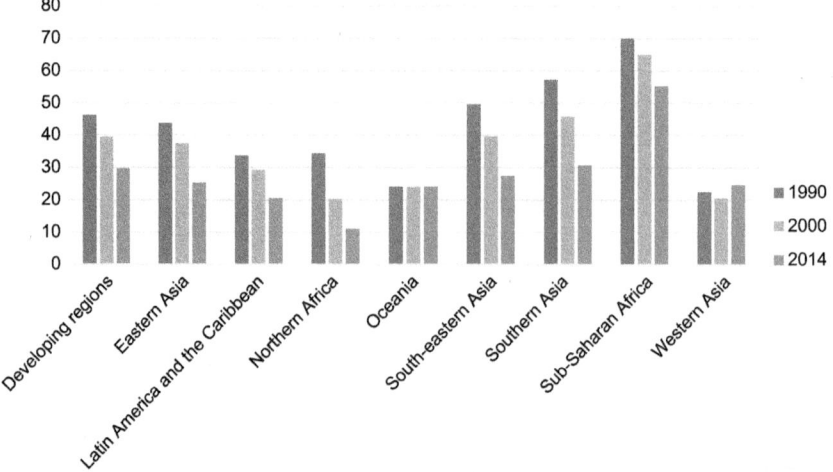

Source: Sustainable Development Goals Database (United Nations Statistics Division, 2016)

Given the high urban population growth projections, especially in rapidly expanding cities in developing countries, the number of global slum dwellers is also expected to keep rising. Any spatial concentration of low-income, unskilled citizens living in informal dwellings in segregated neighborhoods frequently gives rise to a **poverty trap**. The trap forms due to restricted access to jobs, poor infrastructure and urban services, inadequate housing, deteriorating living standards, scarcity and poor quality of public spaces, and often higher crime rates – elements that simultaneously hinder slum upgrading.

Therefore, challenges related to rapid slum development and urban poverty are of critical concern. When city governments fail to deliver basic infrastructure, street networks and municipal services to informal settlements, the associated problems of living in slums – such as poverty, social exclusion, segregation, higher crime rates or health problems – are exacerbated. Concrete actions to address these challenges should be a priority for city managers where slums are on the rise, especially in developing and emerging countries. Examples of strategies include connecting slums to piped water, drainage systems, waste collection and sewer treatments, among other vital actions.

Gentrification

Many neighborhoods in large cities around the world – including New York, London, Berlin, Cape Town or Shanghai – are becoming increasingly unaffordable for working and middle class populations. This trend is driving what is known as **gentrification**.[5] Gentrification is a term that refers to an urban phenomenon in which a neighborhood changes and usually becomes more expensive, due to rising property prices and housing rents and the arrival of new residents with a higher socio-economic status than the current ones. This results in the displacement of incumbent residents, either by choice or by force. At the same time, existing small shops and businesses are often forced to move to cheaper areas. In France, for instance, the share of housing costs in household budgets has increased from 10% in 1960 to 30% in 2010 (European Union, 2011).

The topic of gentrification and its impact on urban areas is often controversial. Gentrification is frequently associated with housing and land speculation, which leads to the disruption of communities and broken

---

[5] The term gentrification was first coined in 1960s by British sociologist Ruth Glass to describe the processes by which working class people were pressed out of parts of London as the middle classes were moving in to areas where they lived.

social networks. This, in turn, deepens social divisions and exclusion in cities, disproportionately affecting lower income residents. Poor and disadvantaged people are often the ones who are pushed out of the city center and the places where they grew up. Finding decent or affordable housing becomes increasingly difficult for them. On the other hand, higher income residents move into the best neighborhoods, which are closer to job opportunities, quality schools, and have the lowest crime rates.

However, **gentrification is a process of transformation and change** in neighborhoods. It happens as a result of advantaged people moving to not-so rich areas, yet it is also the result of government policies and public investments, regarding public transit, and investments in schools or medical centers. Depending on how it is planned and managed, gentrification can also bring positive consequences. In fact, it can be an opportunity for cities to renew deteriorated areas, improve less developed neighborhoods, fill empty spaces with either public spaces, parks or housing, and increase amenities and new services in areas of the city with deficits. Therefore, renewing or newly developing areas of the city can have a positive impact on the quality of life of city dwellers if it does not create forced displacement of incumbent residents, preserves affordable housing, and does not result in greater inequalities and social exclusion.

The real challenge for city managers is to be able to improve housing options, improve conditions in all neighborhoods and create more inclusive cities. In order to tackle the negative consequences of gentrification, some cities have implemented a number of initiatives or regulations. These include: rent control policies, laws requiring to preserve affordable housing, assisting residents displaced by gentrification and/or including a proportion of affordable housing in the creation of new buildings, as we will see in Section 3.

***

2.3 Access to Key Services, Basic Facilities and Infrastructures

As previously mentioned, poverty and inequality are multi-dimensional concepts covering much more than just income and wealth. Improving the access to key resources and services, such as education, health, basic urban infrastructure, adequate housing, basic services (electricity, safe and clean water, ICTs) and transport, are all as important as money-based measures to alleviate the concentration of poverty in certain areas of the city, foster social cohesion and reduce inequalities.

a. Education

Quality education is essential for overcoming poverty and inequality, avoiding exclusion and strengthening social cohesion. When equal opportunities to access quality education are available across the population, this can facilitate upward social mobility, significantly reducing the risk of poverty, diminishing inequalities in the labor market and improving growth prospects. Moreover, education also plays an important role in increasing citizens' participation and in improving respect for diversity and non-discrimination.

Therefore, creating plans to improve the access to quality education and reduce differences in education across the population should be a central goal of any city. First, because **education has the potential to reduce inequality gaps**. And second, due to the fact that **access to education and access to culture are two key components of human capital**, which foster creativity, research and innovation, and act as drivers for economic development and economic growth.[6]

---

[6] Issues of levels of education and access to culture in cities are going to be analyzed in the book volume *Cities and Human Capital.*

b. Health

Healthy populations are essential for equitable and socially inclusive cities, as well as for economic development. Thus, an environment that contributes to health should be available to all sectors of society. However, the growing number of people in urban areas present important challenges for global health: rising air pollution, problems of unsafe water and sanitation, increasing violence, more traffic accidents, and problems of physical inactivity, among others. Therefore, a good and effective health system, as well as the improvement of other factors such as air quality, traffic congestions, water systems, waste management, among others, are essential to achieve safe and healthy cities and citizens.

Despite the fact that health services are usually more often available in cities than in rural areas, **we find important inequalities in the access and use of health services in different groups of society within cities**. For instance, poor children, women, minority groups or people living in informal settlements are more likely to be excluded from health services than other groups of society (Salgado de Snyder et al., 2011). In fact, health inequality in cities is a critical matter since it fuels vicious circles of poverty and exclusion. Health inequality, lack of access to quality education, poverty and living in deprived areas of the city are often correlated.

At the global level, two of the main indicators of good health, life expectancy and child mortality, have improved in recent decades: life expectancy has increased and child mortality has decreased. However, there are significant differences among the populations both within and between cities. **Health inequality is a critical problem in urban areas**. For instance, in a study carried out in different European cities, it was found that neighborhoods with high socio-economic deprivation (understood as percentage of unemployment and blue-collar workers) had a higher excess of mortality in the majority of the cities under study (EUKN, 2014).

Different genetic, social, economic, environmental and cultural factors can affect health. Some are more individual and related to lifestyle, such as diet and physical activity. But in other factors that directly affect health outcomes, cities can play a key role. For instance, city leaders can improve the health of their citizens by improving the environment and air quality of the city, or by providing safe water and sanitation for all, especially in informal settlements, reducing health inequalities. They can also promote healthier behaviors among their populations by building more attractive public spaces that encourage sports and physical activities in all neighborhoods, or by transforming urban mobility schemes into safer and more sustainable transport systems. Lastly, urban leaders can also design healthier and more inclusive cities by increasing coverage of health systems in their cities. Although these are very much dependent on national policies and regulations, local governments can play an important role.

c. Basic Facilities and Infrastructure

As cities grow, so should the basic infrastructure needed to meet the demands of their citizens to achieve a positive quality of life and well-being. Access to adequate housing services and utilities such as water, electricity, gas, sewage, and more recently, the access to internet services and ICTs, as well as a well-connected city's transport infrastructure, are essential for alleviating the concentration of poverty, inequalities and segregation in cities.

Water and Sanitation

Safe, clean water and sanitation are essential for meeting basic human's needs. Conversely, many people around the world still lack access to clean water and sanitation. In 2015, it is estimated that some 663 million people still lack access to improved drinking water globally and about 2.4 billion do not have access to adequate sanitation (WHO/UNICEF, 2015).

Urban populations generally benefit from higher coverage of improved drinking water sources and sanitation in comparison to rural populations. However, rapid population growth and rising urbanization is putting a strain on urban water systems all around the world. In fact, **the demand for water is expected to increase globally by 55% by 2050** (IWA, 2016).

In urban areas, this increasing demand for water is particularly critical in high-dense slums in large cities. Informal settlements often suffer from water scarcity, unsafe or non-potable water, inadequate sanitation and hygienic practices, and poor ventilation. These conditions increase the probability of infectious and chronic diseases and other health issues. For instance, it is estimated that globally over 340,000 children under five years old die annually from diarrheal diseases due to poor sanitation, poor hygiene, or unsafe drinking water (WHO, 2015). As a result, **the absence of improved water and sanitation not only has a direct effect on people's health, but also on social conditions, exacerbating exclusion, poverty and urban health inequality**. Therefore, finding solutions to urban water management challenges are of critical importance.

Energy

As urbanization accelerates, global energy demand increases. This creates two important concerns for municipal leaders around the world: **environmental sustainability** and issues of **affordability and access**. First, energy has a direct impact on the environment. Cities are responsible for more than three quarters of global energy consumption and some 70-80% of greenhouse gas (GHG) emissions worldwide. Thus, they are major contributors to global warming and climate change. In order to solve this critical issue, cities need to create and develop energy efficiency initiatives to deal with climate change and to design urban energy strategies with consideration of their environmental footprint.[7]

---

[7] See book volume *Cities and the Environment* for more information on energy challenges in cities.

Second, urban leaders need to be able to provide the urban infrastructure needed to deliver energy to their citizens. Access to affordable and sustainable energy is crucial to fight urban poverty and promote inclusiveness. **Energy poverty refers to the lack of access to modern energy services, such as electricity or fuel to cook**. Today, some 1.1 billion people globally have no access to electricity (mainly in developing Africa and Asia) and another 2.8 billion only have wood or other biomass for cooking and heating (World Bank, 2016b). The lack of access to energy is a very important issue because it has a direct impact on job opportunities, health, children's education and safety, thus further exacerbating problems of poverty and social exclusion.

Households may not be able to meet their basic domestic energy needs for one of the following two reasons. First, the area where they live may **lack the urban infrastructure** needed to deliver energy, such as the case of people living in slums. Second, many low-income households in cities both in developed and developing countries simply cannot afford to pay for energy, due to the **rising cost of energy bills**. In fact, cities often face a paradox: poor citizens would benefit most from increased building energy efficiency, since this not only improves environmental sustainability and reduces emissions, but also lowers energy consumption, leading to direct savings for households. Yet, low-income citizens cannot afford these investments.

Addressing energy poverty and climate change at the same time will be one of the most critical issues for policymakers all around the world in the decades to come. It will require cooperation between different levels of government, local, regional and national, as well as with other stakeholders. City governments will be key actors in achieving inclusive and sustainable energy systems in urban areas: as the closest political actors to citizens, municipal governments have a critical responsibility to identify which households have a high energy poverty risk, and establish targeted strategies and investments to tackle energy poverty in a more effective way.

New Technologies and Internet

In recent years, new digital technologies have spread to almost every sphere of our personal and professional lives, changing how we live, interact and communicate. For cities, the digital transformation has transformed their economic, social, education, cultural and political processes. The lack of access to ICTs and the internet can have an important impact on the probability of a persons' full participation in the economic, civic and political life of the city. Therefore, an inclusive adaptation to this changing digital environment is critical if city governments do not want to leave some people behind.

The **"digital divide"** of **"digital gap"** refers to the inequalities in access to, use of, or impacts of new technologies between different countries or regions, or between different demographic and socioeconomic groups within a city or urban area. For instance, people living in slums, uneducated people, or older people tend to be more excluded from access to new digital technologies. The issues of the digital divide are very important because they have a direct effect on key areas of inclusion and can be a source of intensifying social inequalities. For instance, a lack of access to the internet might result in not being able to access information regarding new jobs, education or commerce.

As a result, city governments should implement digital initiatives aimed at closing, or at least reducing, the digital divide among their populations with the aim of improving social mobility, economic equality and economic growth. For instance, they should include training programs for people at risk of social exclusion to educate them in the new skills needed to adapt to this changing digital environment. Another possible action is to ensure that fiber networks reach all neighborhoods and all areas of the city, so that no one becomes excluded.[8] **If the right digital initiatives are deployed, ICTs and new technologies can be tools to empower people at risk of exclusion, so they can overcome barriers and gain access to opportunities that otherwise wouldn't be possible**.

Accessibility and Transport

Lastly, accessibility to other services, such as public transport, culture, parks or other urban amenities, are also very important to foster integration and avoid segregation and isolation of some groups of society. In this sense, improving access to safe, affordable, accessible and sustainable **public transport**, the road network and other kinds of mobility (with special attention to the most vulnerable individuals, such as women, disabled or older people) is also crucial to prevent socio-economic inequalities. By improving a city's transport system and bringing citizens in one area of the city closer to amenities in other areas of the city, city authorities can reduce the negative effects of segregation.[9]

***

2.4 Security and Safety

Security and safety are two of the most important matters endangering personal and collective well-being and quality of life in cities. Having **safe urban areas, with low crime rates and levels of violence** should thus be a priority for any city council around the world. City dwellers should feel safe

---

[8] Issues of how new technologies are affecting cities' governance and citizens' lives, as well as some of the indicators used to measure a city's performance with technology, will be further explored in the book volume *Cities and Technology*.

[9] See book volume *Cities and Mobility & Transportation* (Berrone et al., 2016).

to live, work, participate and move around the cities they live in, without fear of harassment, violence or intimidation. However, at the global level, as urbanization accelerates, we find **increasing crime in cities**. In fact, one may say that criminality is increasingly becoming an urban phenomenon, particularly in developing countries with high urbanization rates, great levels of inequality and fragmented societies. On average, **65% of urban dwellers in cities in emerging economies have been victims of some kind of criminal activity** (WEF, 2017).

Table 3: Crime City Index – Top 20 (2017)

#	City, Country	Score	#	City, Country	Score
1	Caracas, Venezuela	86.61	11	Porto Alegre, Brazil	77
2	San Pedro Sula, Honduras	85.59	12	San Salvador, El Salvador	76.19
3	Pietermaritzburg, South Africa	84.23	13	Port Of Spain, Trinidad and Tobago	75.66
4	Fortaleza, Brazil	83.9	14	Sao Paulo, Brazil	72.19
5	Selangor, Malaysia	78.9	15	Detroit, MI, United States	72.09
6	Durban, South Africa	78.58	16	Oakland, CA, United States	71.15
7	Johannesburg, South Africa	78.49	17	Lagos, Nigeria	71.1
8	Recife, Brazil	78	18	Cape Town, South Africa	70.93
9	Pretoria, South Africa	77.99	19	San Juan, Puerto Rico	70.27
10	Rio De Janeiro, Brazil	77.87	20	Kuala Lumpur, Malaysia	69.59

Source: Numbeo (2017).

Note: Crime Index is an estimation of overall level of crime in a given city or a country.

Different factors can contribute negatively to security and safety in cities. First, stark **inequalities, socio-economic diversity and poverty** can play important roles in fueling violence and criminality. Second, **increasing migration flows** have resulted in the cohabitation of diverse cultures and ethnicities within cities. If this diversity is not well managed, it can result in problems of social exclusion and polarization, which is often associated with an increase of conflicts, violence, high levels of street criminality and insecurity. Third, **criminal groups** around certain forms of criminality, such as organized crime, kidnapping and human trafficking, have found it easier to operate in big cities, especially in developing countries with fragile states, with less control and increasing complexity.

Other elements and variables have also added to insecurity and a lack of safe city environments. Urban areas, as centers of population density and political and economic power, have become targets of **international terrorism** from radical armed groups. From the 9/11 attacks on the World Trade Towers in New York (USA) in 2001, to the Mumbai attacks (India) in 2008, to cities in war-zones or unstable states, such as the multiple attacks in Baghdad (Iraq) or Nairobi (Kenya), to European cities as the 2004 bombings in Madrid (Spain), cities around the world have been increasingly hit by terrorism.

Likewise, as cities become more technological and digitalized, **cyber-attacks** can create important threats to local governments and citizens alike. As a result, issues of **digital security** are of rising concern in cities around the world. Lastly, **infrastructure safety,** and in particular road safety, and **health security,** including protection from physical injuries, disease outbreaks and safeguarding from environmental hazards, also play an important role in safety and security in today's metropolises. Consequently, in order to enhance urban safety and security in cities, local governments need to address a variety of factors or dimensions beyond crime and violence. (See Table 4.)

Table 4. EIU Safe Cities Index – Top 20 safest cities (2015)

#	City	Score/100	#	City	Score/100
1	Tokyo	85.63	11	Hong Kong	77.24
2	Singapore	84.61	12	San Francisco	76.63
3	Osaka	82.36	13	Taipei	76.51
4	Stockholm	80.02	14	Montreal	75.6
5	Amsterdam	79.19	15	Barcelona	75.16
6	Sydney	78.91	16	Chicago	74.89
7	Zurich	78.84	17	Los Angeles	74.24
8	Toronto	78.81	18	London	73.83
9	Melbourne	78.67	19	Washington DC	73.37
10	New York	78.08	20	Frankfurt	73.05

Source: The Economist Intelligence Unit (2015).

Note: The index is based on 40 indicators across four dimensions: digital security, health security, infrastructure safety, and personal safety.

City authorities are central to improving urban security and safety. On one hand, through different actions or investments – such as improved connectivity and infrastructure, easy access to different parts of the city, or providing good lighting – cities can prevent crime and reduce the level of insecurity on the streets. On the other hand, by implementing social and economic policies that reduce inequalities and improve social cohesion, urban leaders can reduce the level of polarization within a city and decrease the levels of criminality and insecurity. Lastly, effective coordination between the local government and the local police is essential to improve security within cities.

BOX 2: Social Movements and Protests in Cities and the "Right-to-the-City"

Many cities across the world have witnessed a **significant increase of social movements, strikes, demonstrations, protests and occupation of public spaces** in the past decade: from the 2008-2009 Occupy Wall Street movement across different cities in the US against social and economic inequalities and corporate influences on government; to the Ferguson (Missouri, USA) movement against the spatial segregation and unequal access to opportunities of African-American people, who have been traditionally marginalized; to the Gezi Park protests in Istanbul in 2013 to protect public spaces and against governmental authoritarianism and lack of public consultation; to the 2010 Arab Spring revolutions in cities like Tunis or Cairo; to the Indignados movement in Madrid against anti-austerity measures and political corruption.

Some of these movements and protests are peaceful and non-violent, while others turn violent. When movements and protesters become violent, city authorities must develop strategies to control them and maintain social order, while maintaining the right of freedom of assembly and the right of freedom of speech.

Black live matter movement protest in the US

All of these recent series of protests and social movements in cities around the world are the result of collective urban **citizen's dissatisfaction of many social aspects of cities**, such as exclusion and inequality. Urban dweller around the world are raising their voices around the idea of the "right-to-the-city." The **"right-to-the-city"** is a bottom-up political and cultural movement demanding the right to access urban amenities and make cities more socially just and equitable (Harvey, 2003). The idea behind this movement is that urban societies can build more democratic, sustainable and fair cities if they work collectively to ensure more and better services and opportunities for all; equal access to urban services and resources; more civic participation; and the recognition of cultural diversity and equal rights.

2.5 Social Groups at Higher Risk of Social Exclusion

Poverty, segregation and social exclusion is often concentrated among certain groups of society. Some groups of people with specific socio-demographic characteristics, such as immigrants, ethnic minorities, older people, women, youth, or people with disabilities - and especially for these social groups in low-income households -, are on many occasions excluded from participating in the social, cultural and political life of the city. **When a person is socially excluded, that person has limited capacity to participate in society and often lacks equal prospects to access services and opportunities.** Also, the ability of these social groups to change their position in society and move upward in the social ladder is often very limited.

Therefore, the social and personal economic consequences of being socially excluded, with a higher risk of poverty, are very important. Some of the most crucial social and demographic forces of today, like international migration and ageing populations, might also have an important effect on the economy's growth potential of the city. Nevertheless, the socio-economic, cultural, demographic and ethnic diversity that concentrates in cities must be seen as an opportunity. It can be an enabler of innovation, creativity and growth, instead of a challenge. Finding out how to stimulate the positive aspects of urban diversity and countering the negative ones is essential for exploiting the potential of diversity and achieving socially cohesive urban centers.

a. Migration

Increasing and diversifying migration to cities is one of the most critical demographic trends affecting and changing urban areas across the globe. Migration flows are both the cause and effect of economic development and globalization and they are changing cities' dynamics and levels of social cohesion. Migration is both a national and an international phenomenon. First, inside the same country, individuals may move from rural areas to urban areas, driven by economic and social aspirations. Second, at the international level, people from poorer countries may move to cities in developed countries, looking for better prospects of life for themselves and their families.

International migration in particular has accelerated in the past decades, growing in complexity and reach, **changing population structures and societies** across the globe. In 2015, the number of international migrants worldwide reached 244 million people, up by 41% since 2000 (IOM, 2015a). And cities are the prime recipient of migration flows. **Almost one in five of all migrants live in the world's top 20 largest cities** (IOM, 2015b). In cities like New York, London, Singapore, Sydney or Brussels, more than one-third of the total population is foreign born. (See Figure 5.)

Figure 5: Foreign-born population in selected cities (%)

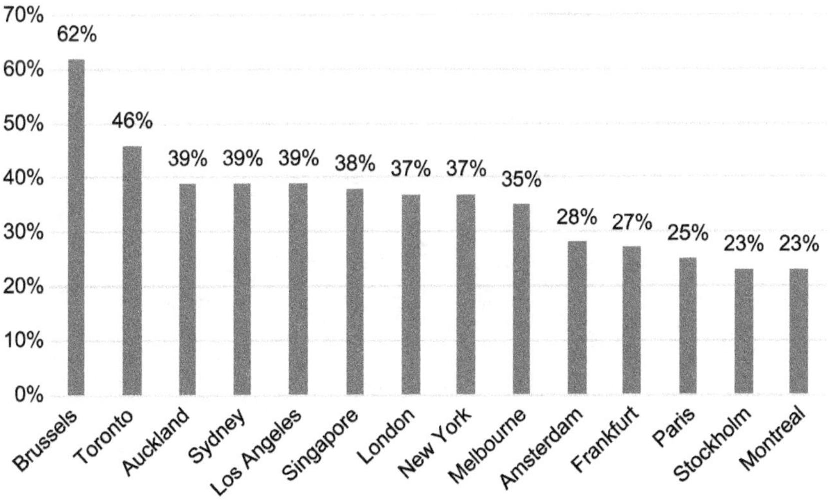

Source: IOM World Migration Report (IOM, 2015b)

In times of crises and instability, increasing immigration in cities has often resulted in problems of **racism and xenophobia**. Immigrants coming from different countries are often blamed for stealing jobs from local people and bringing criminality and insecurity to neighborhoods. As a result, problems of integration and exclusion have resulted from increasing migration flows. Additionally, immigrants often tend to concentrate in a limited number of urban neighborhoods. This is mostly due to their relatively weak position in terms of economic resources and also because of discrimination in the rental housing market. This results in the aforementioned spatial segregation or residential segregation of immigrants and/or ethnic groups, which curtails their access to jobs and opportunities, further exacerbating poverty and exclusion.

However, immigrants vary widely in terms of nationalities, skills, education levels and socioeconomic status. And **this diversity can potentially be a driver for economic growth and social progress**. If city authorities manage this growing cultural diversity in a way that fosters creativity, innovation and development, it can bring positive opportunities both for the economic development of the city and its social and cultural attractiveness.

BOX 3: Parisian Suburbs - Spatial Segregation, Social Exclusion and Riots

Paris and its metropolitan area is one of the most multi-cultural urban areas in Europe: approximately 20% of people living in Paris are immigrants (as of 2013) and 38% of all immigrants in France live in the Paris urban area (2012) (INSEE, 2016a, 2016b). Several waves of immigration arrived to the metropolitan area of Paris in the past century: from Italians, central European Jews, Russians, Spaniards and Portuguese, and lately people originating mainly from Maghreb (particularly Algeria, Morocco and Tunisia), Turkey, and different countries in Sub-Saharan Africa.

Despite this wide diversity, the adaptation of immigrants has been very difficult, especially due to the existence of so-called ethnic ghettos. Some areas in

Greater Paris, such as the Saint Denis department, have significantly high levels of immigration, unemployment and poverty. These isolated and excluded districts have led to socio-economic and ethnic segregation, which has proven to be very problematic, as exhibited by the riots in 2005.

On October 27, 2005 a series of riots started in the Parisian suburb of Clichy-sous-Bois, a district populated by mostly Arab, North African, and black French second-generation immigrants. The riots soon spread to more than 200 towns in the Paris region, as well as to other suburbs in different urban areas of France. In the almost three weeks of rioting, nearly all of the large suburban neighborhoods in France were affected, thousands of vehicles were burned, dozens of public buildings and businesses were set on fire, and at least one person was killed by the rioters. On November 8, 2015, the French government declared a state of national emergency and close to 2,900 rioters were arrested.

These riots were the result of the growing problems of social exclusion, racism, marginalization and lack of employment opportunities affecting the French suburbs, in particular low-income young immigrants or those of immigrant origin. The Paris metropolitan area's social divide show how socio-spatial segregation between wealthy districts and impoverished immigrant districts can trigger problems that lead to social tension, conflict and violence.

b. Ageing Populations

One of the most important trends of the 21st century is the fact that the human population is getting older. Today, people live longer and healthier lives than ever before. In 2015, there were some 901 million people worldwide aged 60 years or over, representing some 12% of the population (UN, 2015). And these numbers are expected to keep growing. According to UN projections, **by 2050 the number of people aged 60 or above is projected to more than double its size,** reaching around 2.1 billion people, or some 21% of global population.

This **undeniable global phenomenon of ageing populations** has been evident in developed countries for quite some time already – for instance, the number of people over 65 years[10] in 2015 in high-income countries was 17% of the total population, in comparison to some 8.2% of the world's total population (World Bank, 2017). But over the past few years, it has started to spread also to the developing world. Now, the ageing of societies is an inexorable trend changing and challenging society structures in countries and cities all around the world.

In the case of cities, the ageing of societies will present critical challenges and implications, since the number of senior citizens is increasingly concentrated in urban areas. **In 2015, 58% of the world's population aged 60 years or above lived in urban areas,** up from 51% in 2000 (UN, 2015). Cities in developing regions, such as Asia, Latin America and Africa, are experiencing the biggest increases in the growth of the number of older persons in urban areas, which is growing faster than in rural areas.[11]

Cities will need to adapt to this demographic shift towards ageing populations in many different ways. First, cities need to cope with the challenge of having an increasingly large non-active population and a reduced tax-base, putting serious pressure on government budgets and finance. Second, city authorities need to adapt infrastructures and urban planning for more age-friendly city designs, such as adapting public transport to elderly requirements and improve accessibility to public spaces. Third, local governments will have to give response to a growing demand for

---

[10] The definitions of older people vary across countries and reports.

[11] At the global level, the number of persons aged 60 years or more increased by 68% in urban areas between 2000 and 2015, compared to a 25% increase in rural areas (UN, 2015).

social services to take care of the elderly, in particular healthcare, and as a result they will have to increase their spending in those services. Lastly, cities will have to tackle specific social cohesion problems more related to the elderly, such as social isolation and loneliness. Older persons are often more vulnerable to exclusion, marginalization and discrimination. For instance, today's information society, in which computer and internet skills are a very important form of participation, are increasing the risk of social exclusion for older people, who often lack the necessary skills and/ or equipment to be included in this new "technology era."

But ageing populations might also provide opportunities to urban environments and urban economies. First, the elderly can make important contributions to cities and societies, by doing volunteer work in their communities and thereby improving social cohesion. For instance, they could help support the inclusion of marginalized groups, such as children at risk of social exclusion or newly arrived immigrants. Second, there are opportunities for new business models and new jobs targeting the needs of the elderly, such as healthcare-related businesses. Local administrations need to implement programs and policies targeted at reducing the social exclusion of older people in cities, and take advantage of the opportunities offered in ageing societies.

c. Women

Women generally face greater discrimination, marginalization and a higher risk of poverty and social exclusion than men. They often have a higher probability of being unemployed or having informal jobs. In particular, poor women living in slums in developing countries tend to find important barriers to access the labor market, and tend to concentrate in low-wage, low-skilled informal sector jobs or/and home-based work. Women and girls also face important difficulties in accessing health, education and other services, as well as to participate safely in the urban public life and in public spaces. Women have a greater risk of insecurity and of experiencing violence.

When around half of the population does not have the same advantages than the other half to live, work and enjoy urban life, significant social cohesion problems follow. To achieve socially cohesive communities and advance social development in cities, **urban leaders need to address issues of gender, such as women's equality, safety, domestic violence and empowerment.** Despite the fact that cities often offer more opportunities to advance gender equality (for instance, in general it is easier for women to access education and to engage in professional activities in urban areas rather than in rural areas), city authorities need to actively engage in actions and policies that ensure the equal participation of women in the social, labor, cultural and political life of the city.

To empower women and achieve gender equality for more cohesive cities, city authorities can act in different areas. First, it is critical to increase the representation of locally elected women and promote the participation of women in local decision-making. In 2015, less than 5% of the world's mayors and 20% of local councilors were women (UCLG, 2015), which shows a clear inequality in women's participation in local decision-making. Second, equal participation of women in the labor market, with equal employment opportunities and equal pay, is also a very important challenge for achieving equality. Third, improving safety in public spaces, as well as enabling the participation of women and girls in public life, is essential. And lastly, tackling violence and insecurity with a special focus on violence against women is necessary for fostering gender equality and reducing women's segregation and exclusion in cities.

d. Youth

Young people are more vulnerable to social exclusion and poverty than many other groups in society. This risk stems from their difficulty in finding stable jobs. The International Labor Organization estimates that the global youth unemployment rate in 2016 was around 13% (ILO, 2016), with **young people approximately two to three times more likely to be unemployed than adults**. Female youth participation rates are even lower than those of male youth.

For cities, the lack of employment opportunities for young people has resulted in underemployment, inequality, problems of social exclusion and lack of equal access to opportunities and services. This has become a critical issue, since most migrants from rural areas to urban areas around the world, especially in developing countries, are young people looking for better opportunities and prospects for life. **High concentrations of youth unemployed in certain areas of cities has led to marginalization and segregation**, resulting in problems of social disorder, insecurity and even violence, particularly in cities in developing countries. Urban managers need to offer equal opportunities and a better quality of life to young people, through inclusive employment policies and strategies. They also need to address issues of equal opportunities and accessibility, such as access to basic utilities and services and housing conditions. In the case of developing cities, tackling issues of youth in slums and street children is particularly critical.

Cities have failed to provide good quality jobs for young people, while urban managers have disappointed them by ignoring their opinions. A survey made to some 15,000 youth aged 15-34 in 34 cities around the world found out that **83% of young people think that their municipal governments are not listening to them**, even though 55% of them would like to participate more in helping building their cities (Youthful Cities, 2016). Since the youngest generations are and will be key actors in the transformation and management of the cities of tomorrow, urban managers must engage youth so they can be actors in building cities and encourage dialogue with them. Youth are well-positioned to take advantage of new opportunities and transformations in cities, such as new urban economies.

Municipal leaders should leverage the opportunities, skills and talents urban youth have to offer. By integrating young people in the economic and political life of the city, urban managers could create economic development in their cities, solve problems of social exclusion, marginalization and poverty, and build sustainability in the cities of tomorrow.

e. Other Vulnerable Groups

Other societal groups are also at a higher risk of social exclusion, marginalization, unemployment and/or poverty. These vulnerable groups include people with disabilities or mental illnesses, LGBT people, individuals with no education or with, at most, lower secondary-level education, or homeless people. Prioritizing investments and initiatives for equal opportunities and integration of all the diverse groups of society will help reduce the inequality gap, marginalization and polarization in cities.

Lastly, it is important to mention that **ensuring civic participation of all citizens**, especially of the abovementioned groups who have a higher risk of social exclusion in all social, cultural and political areas is necessary for ensuring equal rights and opportunities, while enhancing social interactions.[12]

---

[12] Issues of public participation and civic engagement will be analyzed in more detail in the book volume *Cities and Governance*.

3. Inclusive and More Equitable Urban Development: Best Practices and Case Studies

While the challenges to social cohesion in cities are many and varied, as seen in the previous section, the changing socio-economic and demographic realities, as well as the increasing heterogeneity and diversity in cities, also offer new opportunities to create urban areas that are more inclusive, cohesive and with greater access to more services and opportunities, together with positive effects on economic performance and social mobility. This section explores policies, initiatives and programs that local governments around the world have implemented in order to build and strengthen social cohesion and community engagement in their cities.

As mentioned in the other volumes of this series, a number of levers of change are enabling cutting-edge transformations in the way cities function and how their citizens interact among each other and with the government. We have defined a **framework of analysis** with these main "levers of change" or "dimensions of action" to help us understand and analyze how they interrelate among each other and to help city governments and urban managers identify solutions to overcome urban challenges and define and implement urban management plans. The overall framework is presented in Figure 6.

Figure 6: Smart urban management model

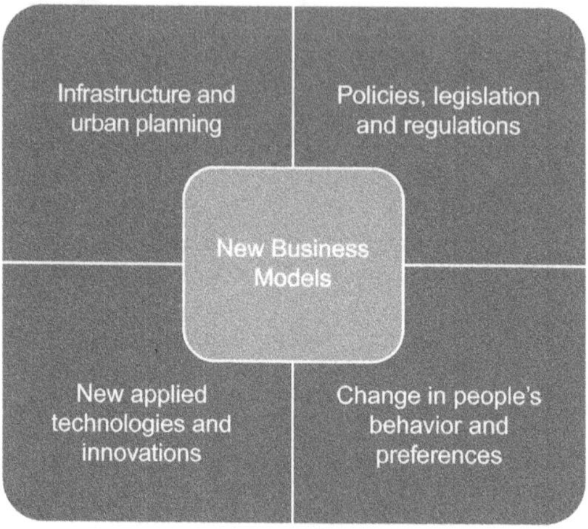

Source: Prepared by the authors.

In the case of social cohesion, all these levers of change play a critical role. First of all, <u>infrastructure and urban design</u> are key instruments for reducing urban inequalities and promoting accessibility and opportunities. As mentioned before, the spatial distribution of a city is highly related to the probability of being at risk of social exclusion. By strengthening inclusive urban planning and design, the difficulties to access certain parts of the city, urban services, public spaces and affordable housing can be reduced.

Second, local institutions have at their disposal many different mechanisms, <u>policies, legislations and regulations</u> that can have a direct or indirect effect on the opportunities offered to their citizens, as well as promote well-being and inclusion in cities. In this sense, explicit and direct initiatives aimed at boosting social inclusion can create more harmonious and cohesive communities and enable social progress. Due to the fact that city governments are closer to citizens, they are often better positioned to understand the concrete challenges of their citizens and give a more tailored and effective response to problems related to unemployment, migration, poverty, among others. But other less direct institutional mechanisms, such as a well-functioning democratic system and the rule of law (with less corruption, a fair and equal judicial system, etc.) can also have important effects on inclusion and exclusion processes. **Addressing inequality and social exclusion requires political will, good institutions and well-defined and well-targeted social policies and legislations**.

Third, change in people's preferences and behaviors, as well as changing demographic structures is also having an important effect in the planning and functioning of urban areas. As mentioned at the beginning of Section 2, social inclusion in cities and communities is also about a "sense of belonging" and "integration" in society. As globalization and urbanization accelerates, we find growing diversity in cities (in socio-economic, cultural, demographic and ethnic terms). It is important that multiculturalism, diversity and non-discrimination are incorporated equally in this "sense of belonging." Likewise, local authorities and communities must work together to strengthen social cohesion, social capital (trust, participation, solidarity, social networks) and reduce violence, so a sense of integration, belonging and social justice is achieved.

Fourth, new technologies and innovations have the potential to bring important opportunities and respond to specific social cohesion challenges in various policy fields and sectors, as well as to help break down integration barriers. For instance, in health and education, advances in ICTs will facilitate new and more inclusive solutions. They can also help improve the efficiency of basic urban services and infrastructure, such as water systems or electric grids, and create safer and more comfortable urban environments, reducing criminality and social disorder. Lastly, new business models that integrate all the previous elements in a holistic way can increase social cohesion. For instance, new business models in the healthcare and education sectors can help reduce inequality and poverty in cities.

Local and regional governments need to take action and implement active inclusion policies at the local and regional level in order to alleviate the negative socio-economic side effects of urbanization and maximize the potential opportunities brought by urban diversity. As we have seen, social challenges, such as poverty, social exclusion and inequality, are very much intertwined and reinforce each other. They are also interlinked with other economic and environmental challenges in urban areas. As a result, **city governments need to take a holistic approach to social cohesion that integrates the different social, economic and environmental dimensions**.

This section is going to focus on the initiatives, strategies and policies that urban governments can implement to achieve this goal. We will describe some examples of best practices and case studies regarding the improvement of social cohesion in cities around the world. These include urban planning and the development of transport infrastructure to prevent spatial segregation; social policies to fight inequalities and poverty; the provision of a good legal and regulatory framework for developing new social business models; the socio-economic integration of immigrants and other groups of society at higher risk of social exclusion; improving the access to more and better jobs; among others. For each solution, the main levers of change that play a key role for that particular best practice will be highlighted. However, it is important to keep in mind that all these "dimensions of action" function in conjunction and that they need to be understood as part of a single engine that works as one. Also, it is important to mention that actions between the local governments and national and regional governments need to be coordinated to ensure complementarities and achieve inclusiveness in urban areas.

***

3.1 Spatial Inclusion and Access to Basic Urban Infrastructure

When a group of residents are excluded from equal access and opportunities that the city has to offer, integration and social cohesion problems arise. Local governments need to identify spatial strategies that can discourage segregation and ensure access to basic services, so that no group is excluded. To achieve urban inclusion and reduce social and spatial inequalities, municipalities across the globe need to take a comprehensive urban policy approach that improves access to affordable housing, and ensures basic urban services and infrastructures, while implementing social policies to reduce poverty and inequality.

3.1.1 Slums Upgrading

Many low-income households, especially in developing countries, tend to cluster in some parts of the city in informal settlements or slums. As previously mentioned, slums usually lack adequate housing and they have limited infrastructure provisions and services. Access to safe water, adequate sanitation, waste collection or electricity can be a daily struggle for many disadvantages homes living in them. As a result, slums become centers of urban poverty and exclusion.

To improve this situation, local governments need to take effective action and develop inclusive and integrated policies that avoid spatial segregation and alleviate the concentration of urban poverty and inequality in some parts of the city. **Slum upgrading and improved accessibility through informal settlements policies** are key to sustainable urbanization and stronger social cohesion in cities, especially in developing countries.

Infrastructure and
urban planning

Policies, legislation
and regulations

BEST PRACTICE: RIO DE JANEIRO
- Favela Bairro slum upgrading program

Rio de Janeiro is the second most populous city in Brazil, and the sixth most populous in the Americas, with some 6.4 million people in an area of 1,200 km². Additionally, some 12 million peo-ple live in the metropolitan area of Rio. The city is home to different ethnic groups, including people of Portuguese ancestry (as a re-sult of being a former Portuguese colony); blacks (whose ancestors were brought to Brazil as slaves); *pardos* or multiracial people; and Asian and Amerindian people to a lesser degree. Rio is a major economic and cultural center. Its GDP in 2011 was some $200 bil-lion and it is the headquarters of many companies. Culture is an im-portant part of the city, with a creative vibrant scene. Moreover, it is one of the most visited places in the world. In 2012, UNESCO declared the whole of Rio a World Heritage Site.

Rio de Janeiro, Brazil

Source: Pixabay, CC0.

Context

- Like many other big cities in developing countries, Rio de Janeiro has faced a critical problem of rapid unplanned urbanization. Since the end of the 19th century, when the first slum was founded in Rio, low-income populations have settled in different *morros* (hills) of the city, giving rise to a large number of informal settlements, known in the city as "*favelas.*"

- *Favelas* are often constructed with little planning and traditionally have lacked access to basic infrastructure, such as safe water, electricity and public ser-vices. Additionally, they have been hubs of poverty, exclusion, marginalization and crime. Many drug dealers used to live in *favelas*.

- In contrast, high-income residents usually live by the sea and not in the hills. This has resulted in a unique urban contrast in the city that reflects Rio's particularly unequal economic and social structure. In fact, inequality in the city is one of the highest in the world. In recent decades, the GINI Index in Rio has been between 0.60-0.50, reflecting high socio-economic disparities.

- Rio's *favelas* have more residents than any other Brazilian city. In the 1990s, around 1 million people lived in over 500 *favelas* in Rio de Janeiro's *morros*, representing about 16% of the city's population (Lucci, Bhatkal, Khan and Berliner, 2015). More recent estimates suggest that close to 1.5 million – or around 23-24% of the city's population – live in some 1,000 *favelas* (Catalytic Communities, 2015). However, it is very difficult to known exactly how many people live in them.

- These slums vary greatly in terms of size, building quality, density, etc. However, some common characteristics can be found: illegality in land titling or property, the lack of urban infrastructure, the precariousness of home conditions and segregation from the formal town (Magalhães and di Villarosa, 2012).

Actions

- Over the past few decades, different initiatives have been conducted to improve quality of life in the city's *favelas*.

- The first large-scale and best-known slum upgrading program is the *Favela Bairro* program. It was set up in 1994 with the final aim to integrate the *favelas* into the city by providing urban infrastructure, services and social policies. The program was initially targeted at *favelas* with between 500 and 2,500 households.

- *Favela Bairro* has been implemented in three phases: Phase I (1994-2000), Phase II (2000-2007) and Phase III (2012-present), also known as *Morar Carioca*. The *Favela Bairro* program aimed at being a multi-sectoral initiative, tackling different issues at the same time. Phase I and II focused on improving the living conditions of families living in *favelas* by providing basic infrastructure (water, sewerage, drainage, street lighting, street paving, parks and sport areas, reforestation); increasing social services (childcare centers; social-service centers; education; health; etc.); community engagement; and land titling (IDB, 2011).

- Funding of the project comes from the local government and the Inter-American Development Bank (IDB): Phase I and Phase II have invested US$600 million, of two different contracts of US $300, with $180 million from IDB and $120 million from the City Government of Rio de Janeiro; Phase III is based on investment of another $300 million, with $150 million coming from IDB and $150 million from the City Hall (Secretaria Municipal de Habitação, n.d.).

- The program is a multi-level collaboration, between the Municipality of Rio de Janeiro, the national government and the IDB, and is carried out in close collaboration with local communities. It is led by the Municipal Housing Department (Secretaria Municipal de Habitação), in alliance with a technical committee and neighborhoods associations.

- *Morar Carioca,* the latest slum upgrading program, aims to formalize and integrate all of the City's *favelas* by 2020, benefiting up to 232,000 households (C40, 2013). This phase of the program, besides upgrading and maintenance of informal settlements, has added a safety component, introducing special police in *favelas* and setting up Units of Pacifying Police (UPP). It also aims to create public spaces to promote social cohesion.

- Additionally, other programs such as *Minha Casa, Minha Vida* in Rio, have also helped low-income families improve their own homes and reduce the housing deficit in Brazil. *Minha Casa, Minha Vida* (translated as *My House, My Life*) is an income transfer program launched by the Federal Government in 2009 and implemented by Caixa, the country's third largest bank. It is aimed at helping low income households to build and upgrade their housing by providing access to credit and support (families earning up to 10 minimum wages are eligible to participate).

Outcomes

- The *Favela Bairro* program provides a best practice for slum upgrading. Although it also had some failures, the program was successful in decreasing inequality among slum residents and reducing economic and spatial segregation within treated neighborhoods (Atuesta and Soares, 2016).

- By the end of the second phase of the *Favela Bairro* program, some 100 *favelas* had received upgrades (38 favelas by the end of the first phase and more than 60 in the second phase of the program), with some 137,000 households benefited from it (Lucci et al., 2015; Osborn, 2012).

- Access to basic urban services, such as water, sanitation and waste collection, public lighting and street network, have increased significantly for the *favelas* within the program in comparison to non-participating *favelas*. For instance, after Phase I and II, 81% of *favelas* in the program were connected to the water system, in comparison to 55% of non-treated settlements (IDB, 2011). In Phase II, 9,890 public lighting points were installed and began functioning (Magalhães and di Villarosa, 2012).

- Improvements in transportation and mobility have also been achieved, such as the creation of a cable car system in one of the largest *favelas* in Rio, the *Complexo do Alemao*.

Complexo do Alemao favela from Rio's cable car

Photo: Ana Duch

- In relation to education, employment and income, results on the first two phases of the program showed a small but statistically significant impact on school attendance among those aged 5-20 years old, and a 15% increase in household incomes (IDB, 2011).

- Due to general improvements and security tenure regulations (people who lived on a parcel of land for more than five years received some security against eviction), property values and housing prices have increased. However, reg-ularizations of land tenure or property titling still remain an important issue to be resolved. Despite property titling being part of the original program, it was never implemented due to some legal and logistic difficulties (Atuesta and Soares, 2016).

- As a result of the country's slum upgrading programs, as well as other national social programs such as the *Bolsa Familia* Program, many low-income Brazilians have been able to move from the lower class to the middle class.

- However, despite all the improvements (especially in regards to access to infrastructure and services), full integration of the *favelas* into the city has not yet been achieved. Additionally, income inequality today is still very high in the city and the metropolitan area.

- In general, there has been public support for the program over time (Lucci et al., 2015). However, the program has also had some critics. Debated issues include house price increases and gentrification; land titling; the need for a more active role among communities in designing social policies beyond housing and infrastructure; and the difficulty of maintenance.

- Strong municipal government commitment was key for the program's success. Additionally, coordination and cooperation with other stakeholders, the national government and local communities was also found to be essential.

- The program is considered a model project by the United Nations. Additionally, it received an award at the Expo 2000 in Hannover (Germany), and in 2013 the *Morar Carioca* program (the third phase of the project) won the Sustainable Communities award of C40 Cities Awards. Therefore, there has been international recognition of the program.

New business models

Change in people's behavior and preferences

BOX 4: Turning Slums' Waste Collection Problem into an Opportunity

In the 1990s, Cono Norte was one of the largest slums in Lima, Peru's capital, with some 1.5 million inhabitants. Cono Norte generated some 1,000 tons of garbage a day, with less than half of it collected by municipal workers (Albert, Werhane, and Rolph, 2014). This was creating serious environmental issues and health problems for the citizens.

Albina Ruiz, a young student horrified by the piles of garbage in the city, decided to write her thesis on **microenterprises and environmental sanitation** in Cono Norte, Lima. After that, she decided to develop it as a financially viable and sustainable business that would solve the problem and engage poor communities. She developed a **new model of solid waste management** that was inclusive and environmentally sustainable. The model engages micro-entrepreneurs in poor communities, in particular unemployed people, to take charge of collecting and processing garbage for low service fees. It is supported by creative marketing and educational programs to persuade families to use the services and pay for them. As a result, it encourages participation and tries to **change behavior and encourage sustainable waste management** (Skoll, 2015). On average, a family could earn some $160 for recycling paper, more than the minimum wage (Albert et al., 2014).

In 2002 she founded *Ciudad Saludable* (healthy city), a non-profit organization to manage and promote the waste management model. The program was very successful and was expanded to many other cities in Peru, as well as other countries, including Colombia, Mexico, Brazil, Peru, Venezuela, Bolivia, Dominican Republic, and even India and Egypt. *Ciudad Saludable* has received numerous awards, including the 2006 Skoll Award, the 2008 Energy Globe Award, the Clean Amazon Award in 2009 and the Fairness Award in 2011. By 2012, the enterprise had over 1,500 waste collectors and had improved the lives of millions of impoverished people living in slums (Albert et al., 2014).

Ciudad Saludable provides a good example of a business model designed to help the development of the green economy and promote public policies focusing on solid waste management, while helping people at risk of poverty and exclusion.

***

3.1.2 Affordable Housing and Gentrification

In developed countries, informal settlements or slums are not that common, but access to adequate, safe and affordable housing is a critical issue. Rising housing costs and low-income residents' displacement due to gentrifying neighborhoods is an important challenge for cities around the world. Local governments need to implement strategies and policies to ensure affordable housing for all and protect low-income residents from gentrification.

City leaders can take action to maintain affordability and diversity in their cities through different policy tools, such as: coordinating land use; community land trusts; investing in public housing; providing support to finance housing; reducing or freezing property taxes to long-time residents; influencing housing demand through rent control; or helping residents at risk of displacement with anti-harassment laws, among many other actions. However, it is important to keep in mind that there is no single effective strategy and local governments should adapt to their specific own realities and needs.

Infrastructure and urban planning

Policies, legislation and regulations

BOX 5: Inclusionary Zoning to Promote Affordable Housing

Inclusionary Zoning (IZ), also called inclusionary housing, refers to a set of local programs or ordinances that have been developed in different U.S. cities to promote affordable housing for low, moderate or middle-income households in new residential developments. IZ can either incentivize or require the creation of affordable housing along with new housing development. IZ programs vary widely depending on the city: they can be voluntary or mandatory; target different income levels; or they can require affordable units to be permanently affordable or allow affordability to expire (such as in Boston , where IZ policies require houses to be affordable only up to 50 years) (Herrine, Yager, and Mian, 2016).

By way of example, we will exhibit the IZ policies of New York City and Washington DC. New York is one of the cities that has developed different Inclusionary Housing Programs (IHP) in recent decades. The first two programs, the R10 program in 1987 and the Inclusionary Housing Designated Areas (IHDA) program in 2005 were only voluntary programs that provided bonuses for the construction or preservation of permanent affordable housing units (City of New York, 2016). However, since 2016 a new Mandatory Inclusionary Housing Program has been approved to ensure affordable housing to low- and moderate-income households and foster more economically diverse communities. The new policy is now mandatory and permanent with different levels of affordability including 25% of residential areas reserved for affordable housing units for residents with incomes averaging 60% AMI (average median income) and 30% for citizens with incomes averaging 80% AMI (City of New York, 2016).

Another example is the U.S. capital. Washington D.C. approved its first IZ policy in 2006 for households with income of up to 80% of area median family income (MFI) and the first units appeared in 2011. The DC IZ policy requires new housing developments to reserve 8-10% of them to be rented or sold below market rate units. In return, home builders can build 20% more housing to compensate the cost (Coalition for Smarter Growth, 2016). To be more inclusive and meet the real needs of the poor, as of 2016, the D.C. Zoning Commission agreed that most new residential developments provide IZ rental units affordable at 60% of MFI, and all for-sale homes at 80% median family income.

Washington DC

Source: Pixabay, CC0

However, the success of inclusionary zoning policies is not yet very clear. Some studies have found that these policies do help prevent housing prices from raising in gentrifying neighborhoods, but they also found that IZ policies don't automatically make housing more affordable for very low-income families (Stromberg and Sturtevant, 2016).

***

3.2 Fighting Poverty and Inequality: Equal Opportunities for All

Poverty and inequality are concentrated in cities. But urban areas can also be engines for poverty reduction and economic development. Local governments have at their disposal initiatives and programs that can contribute to increasing opportunities and overall prosperity. For instance, by improving accessibility to jobs and employment, facilitating access to education and skills building, and implementing pro-poor economic development initiatives, urban administrations can achieve poverty reduction and the inclusion of marginalized groups of the society.

3.2.1 Education

Although this issue is going to be examined in the book volume *Cities and Human Capital,* due to the importance of education for reducing poverty and inequality, it is necessary to also mention it here. **Education and training help drive economic growth, alleviate poverty and enhance social cohesion**. In fact, equal access to education and training, which develops new skills, plays a critical role in social and income mobility in cities.

Local governments need to ensure that all children have access to equitable and quality education. Lack of education and skills hinders the number and quality of economic opportunities, especially for the urban poor and disadvantaged. It also hampers social inclusion. Rapid technological changes and urbanization growth are changing the composition of employment. As new skills are demanded in the labor market, cities need to adapt their education systems to the changing dynamics of the job market and provide education and training that enables the development of these skills.

New applied technologies and innovations

Change in people's behavior and preferences

BOX 6: New Technologies that Make Learning More Available and Accessible for the Poor

In 1999, the Indian Professor Sugata Mitra decided to conduct an experiment, known as "Hole in the Wall", in order to investigate different forms of learning under unsupervised environments. Prof. Mitra embedded an internet-connected computer within a wall in a slum in Kalkaji, New Delhi, so that children in the slum could use it freely and experiment with it. Without any previous knowledge or formal training, children learned how to use the computer and then taught each other. Researchers observed that, in addition to becoming computer literate, children were able to teach themselves sufficient English for using search engines and email, and they improved their mathematics and science results in schools.

The results of the experiment showed that without supervision and formal teaching, children can teach themselves and each other. Prof. Sugata called this Minimally Invasive Education (MIE). Since then, the experiment has been repeated in many different places.

In 2013, Prof. Mitra won the TED Prize award of $1 million, which allowed him to create the School in the Cloud (www.theschoolinthecloud.org). The School in the Cloud project aims to help students take control of their own learning and create an environment where children, no matter how rich or poor, can engage and connect with information and mentoring online. The project now includes eight physical locations or labs (five in India, two in the UK and one in New York, USA). The labs' main objective is to offer an environment where a global community of educators can learn the impact of self-organized learning environments (SOLE) on children from different educational backgrounds just with computers and Internet connection.

This experiment is a good example of how using new technology in basic education can improve access and quality of learning and education for children with minimum resources and at risk of poverty and exclusion.

Children in India

Source: Pixabay, CC0

***

3.2.2 Innovative Business Models

Cities and countries across the globe can also overcome poverty and inequality **in cooperation with the private sector through innovative business models**. There is an opportunity for the private sector to build inclusive businesses that create shared value, increase employability, improve services and generate new economic activities for the poor.

a. Social Innovations

As we have seen in the previous section, the number and complexity of social challenges in cities is huge. In order to find solutions to these complex social problems, a number of initiatives at the local level are being developed. One of them is *Social Labs* or *Social Innovation Labs*, which consists of platforms aimed at bringing together different sectors of society (government, civil society, businesses, etc.) to think, work and experiment in order to co-create solutions. Additionally, *social entrepreneurs* and *social start-ups* in cities around the world are developing innovative businesses to find solutions to social challenges and maximize the social impact of their businesses.

New business models

Change in people's behavior and preferences

BOX 7: Towards a More Sustainable Food System

As global population and urbanization increase, the way people produce, buy and market food will change. Despite progress in recent decades, about 793 million people are undernourished globally, particularly in developing countries (FAO, 2015). At the same time, some people are at risk of diseases due to over-consumption of food. Some 33-50% of all food produced globally is never eaten and is thrown away. In fact, **the value of wasted food is worth over $1 trillion** (OLIO, 2016). Additionally, the sustainable production of food is a critical issue, since the global food system affects and is affected by the environment and climate change.

Therefore, finding solutions to the challenges of the food system is very important. With this aim, different social initiatives have emerged around the world. For instance, the *Sustainable Food Lab* is a social lab and global network that seeks to generate a more sustainable food system. It is a platform for innovation in the global food system that brings together corporate food companies, civil society organizations, farmers and government officials to solve this pressing challenge. It provides advice on sustainability strategy and programs, collaboration projects and leadership development.

Another example of an innovative initiative in the food system is the OLIO app, a food-sharing app aimed at fighting wasted food. The app connects people with their neighbors, local shops, cafés and markets within a geographical area in order to share surplus food or donate it to charity, so that it is not thrown away. The app was launched in 2015 for only five postcode areas in North London. As of March 2017, OLIO was operable in over 40 countries.

b. Improved Access to Credit and Finance

Making financial services accessible to the urban poor and the disadvantaged has the potential to create opportunities for low-income residents, empower vulnerable groups of society and help entrepreneurs develop and expand their businesses. Creating and facilitating financial markets that are available for all, including the poor, can lead to inclusion and social cohesion in cities.

New business models

New applied technologies and innovations

BOX 8: M-Pesa, Mobile Phone Technology to Enhance Financial Inclusion

With the aim of taking advantage of the spread of mobile phones and help citizens' access to financial services, M-Pesa was developed. The project was launched in Kenya in 2007 by Vodafone for Safaricom, a leading communications company and mobile network, with operations in East and Central Africa. M-Pesa is a mobile phone-based money service, which allows users to store, withdraw and transfer money, while also providing other financial services, such as payments of goods and services, credit, insurance and pensions. The system is simple to access and operate and the costs are cheap.

Through a network of agents at small-time vendors in kiosks and shops, M-Pesa allows customers to deposit and withdraw money. The number of "M-Pesa agents" is much higher than the number of traditional banks. This has significantly increased access to money and other financial services, since most Kenyans didn't have the opportunity to access to traditional banks before, especially low-income residents, people living in slums in big cities like Nairobi and/or people living in rural areas. In fact, access to formal financial services increased from 26% of Kenya's bankable population in 2006 to 67% in 2013 (Muthiora, 2015). Therefore, **the system has enhanced financial inclusion of social groups at a higher risk of marginalization and exclusion.**

Policymakers can help enabling financial inclusion. Although this is a private sector initiative, cooperation with the Central Bank of Kenya (CBK) to create the **basic legal and regulatory framework** for the business model to succeed has been key. Besides, even though this has been a business model used through the country, it has had a great effect on cities too. For instance, in Nairobi, the capital and creative hub of Kenya, the growth in digital entrepreneurship has grown exponentially since the launched of M-Pesa, with a proliferation of innovation hubs and digital startups using its services (Muthiora, 2015). Therefore, mobile money and access to financial services has had a positive impact in the digital and technological entrepreneurship scene of the city.

As of September 2016, M-Pesa had some 25 million registered customers in Kenya, with more than 17 million active customers and 114,000 M-Pesa agents (Safaricom Limited, 2017). Moreover, it is estimated that M-PESA contributed Kshs. 184 billion to the Kenyan economy (excluding transaction fees). Additionally, a study by MIT and Georgetown University found that since 2008, M-PESA increased daily per capita consumption levels of 194,000 families, or 2% of Kenyan households, taking them **out of extreme poverty** (living on less than $1.25 per day) (Matheson, 2016). In particular, female-headed households experienced greater increases in consumption than male-headed households. Therefore, it has also been a **gender inclusive initiative**.

M-Pesa is an example of how mobile-based money services can have a positive impact on reducing poverty in developing countries by using mobile technologies that give access to financial services to many unbanked low-income people. Moreover, it has facilitated the creation of new small businesses and start-ups. Moreover, M-Pesa has also cut down on corruption by reducing the need to operate with cash.

Source: Pixabay, CC0

***

3.3 Building Integration and Inclusion

The integration and participation of all groups of people, in particular those with a higher risk of social exclusion and marginalization, is essential for building socially cohesive societies. By fostering community-driven development, citizen engagement and participation, urban governments will be able to achieve more inclusive, fair, equitable and prosperous cities for all.

3.3.1 Diverse Communities

As a result of international migration, city populations are increasingly diverse in terms of ethnicities, nationalities, religion and culture. As previously mentioned, increasing diversity can be a source of innovation, economic development and wealth creation and, if managed properly, it can reduce discrimination. However, **diversity does not mean integration**. Avoiding the creation of ethnic ghettos is essential to achieve social cohesion. Although successful integration depends very much on national policies, **city governments have a prominent role governing diversity**. Due to the fact that they are closer to these diverse societies, local governments are often better prepared to give response to the negative effects of diversity, while taking advantage of the potential opportunities offered by diversity as a driver for innovation, growth and social progress.

Policies, legislation and regulations

BEST PRACTICE: AMSTERDAM
— Managing Diversity to Build Social Cohesion

Amsterdam is the capital and the largest city of the Netherlands. In 2016, the city had a population of some 835,000 inhabitants. Additionally, above two million people lived in the Amsterdam Metropolitan Area. The Dutch capital is an important economic, commercial, political, cultural and touristic center. Many multinational companies have their headquarters in the city and it is one of the top financial centers in Europe. Its seaport is one of the most important of the country and of Europe. Moreover, Amsterdam is known as one of the most bicycle-friendly cities in the world, with more bikes than permanent residents as of August 2016 (Iamsterdam, 2016).

Amsterdam, The Netherlands

Source: Pixabay, CC0.

Context

- The Netherlands has been an important destination for immigrants since the 17th and 18th century, when it was a center of trade and shipping.

- In particular, Amsterdam's diversity is almost as old as the city itself.

- However, since the 1950s, Amsterdam has experienced an increased influx of people originating from many different countries, with two main migration flows: one from former colonies, such as Suriname, Indonesia, and Antillean islands like Aruba, Curaçao and St. Martin; and another flow from countries such as Turkey and Morocco.

- Although Amsterdam society has generally been considered open and tolerant, this intensified international migration has at times resulted in ethnic tensions, and recently, in increased racism and xenophobia.

- Today, the capital of the Netherlands is **one of the most diverse and multicultural cities** in the world with residents form around 180 different nationalities and 45% ethnic minorities (Iamsterdam, 2017).

- According to statistics, as of 2016, 48.3% of the city's population is Dutch and 51.7% is foreign, called "*allochtonen*", which refers to a person who has at least one foreign-born parent (CBS, 2017).

Actions

- National policies concerning immigration and diversity have been historically tolerant since the 1970s, focusing on different fields, from "minority policies" to "integration policies" (van Heelsum, 2008). In fact, Article 1 of the Dutch Constitution bans discrimination based on a person's beliefs, race or sexual preferences.

- More precisely, the City of Amsterdam has historically tried to be a leader for these policies. In 1989 the City published its first "Frame Document Municipal Minority Policy" to set up extra facilities for ethnic minority groups and stop discrimination and racism (van Heelsum, 2008).

- Since then, the city has dedicated extensive policies, funds and initiatives to fighting discrimination and to avoid the creation of ghettos in the city. In 1996 the Municipality added its own code of conduct for local authority staff to the abovementioned Article 1 of the Constitution, along with a complaints scheme and an anti-discrimination office (Iamsterdam, 2017).

- Additionally, in 1999, with the aim of developing a more inclusive policy, embracing different kinds of people, lifestyles, religions and beliefs, the Municipality formulated a "diversity policy," targeting not only immigrants, but also people of foreign descent, women, the disabled and homosexuals (van Heelsum, 2008).

- The city council now has five advisory bodies to support it in its migrants' policy. It also has specific policies for the emancipation of women and it applies an active policy to fight against discrimination of the LGBT community.

- In order to support the participation and integration of all ethnic minorities, including immigrants and refugees, as well as to address growing racism and xenophobia, the Dutch capital has undertaken positive action through different mechanisms and programs. For instance, in order to solve the under representation of immigrants among the staff of the public administration, a mechanism has been introduced aimed at recruiting non-Dutch people or Dutch people with foreign origins to work in the public service. As of 2011, the target was 27% (European Union, 2011). This initiative has been implemented with the goal of ensuring that the civil service better reflects the population's diversity and the ethnic composition of the city.

- Another example is the participation of the City of Amsterdam as a partner of the *Suikeroom* project, a fund for ethnic start-up companies (to solve their lack of connections and networks), financed by established companies (Moloney and Kirchberger, 2010).

- Additionally, the project group on refugees develops specific policies on integration obligation, language, housing, (un)employment, healthcare and financial issues (Blom, 2014). The budget for the different projects and activities comes from the municipality itself, the European Union and the national government, depending on the initiative.

- More recently, in 2016, the City of Amsterdam, together with other partners (Amsterdam Marketing, AmsterdamFM, Bridgizz, Nieuwwij, Story Supply, the OBA (Amsterdam Public Library), the Amsterdam Museum and Het Parool) initiated the **180 Amsterdammers** initiative. This initiative aims at celebrating diversity and increasing the sense of belonging for diverse populations by mapping all of the current 180 nationalities living within Amsterdam, with photographs and stories of them.

Outcomes

- Amsterdam is a major city with decades of experience carrying out positive immigration and diversity policies. With some half of the city's population born abroad or with parents or (great) grandparents born abroad, managing diversity, integration and inclusion amid increasing racism and xenophobia is and will continue to be increasingly important to achieve social cohesion.

- According to the *Burgermonitor 2015*, 85% of Amsterdammers feel connected to the city, thus experiencing a sense of belonging. This percentage has grown from 80% in 2011 and is higher than in the rest of the Netherlands. Additionally, about half of the Amsterdammers feel connected with his or her district, and almost three-quarters with their neighborhood (Gemeente Amsterdam, 2016). Moreover, half of the Amsterdammers reported generally positive interactions between different groups in the city.

- However, about two-thirds of the respondents in the aforementioned survey stated that they had experienced discrimination on the basis of origin or skin color at some point (Gemeente Amsterdam, 2016).

- The Diversity Program among the staff of the public administration achieved some progress in the first years of implementation, moving from 14% of staff with a migrant background in 2006 to some 22% in 2008 (Moloney and Kirchberger, 2010).

- As we have seen, the political commitment of the City of Amsterdam to support diversity and equality has been key. The framing of migration and diversity in Amsterdam has been predominantly positive. However, more concrete policies on some issues may be needed in the future.

Iamsterdam

Source: Pixabay, CC0

- Despite all the described actions to achieve the integration of diverse groups, in the past decade the Netherlands has experienced the emergence of right-wing political parties demanding more restrictive measures on migration, such as an integration exam.

a. Integration of Refugees

The world is currently experiencing the worst refugee crisis since World War II. The severe geopolitical crisis, instability and wars in countries in the Middle-East and Africa have resulted in an unprecedented surge in migration. Refugees, asylum seekers and displaced people usually settle in cities, where they find better job prospects and opportunities, as well as social networks. In fact, **over 60% of the world's 19.5 million refugees and 80% of 34 million internally displaced people (IDPs) live in urban areas** (UNHCR, 2017).

As a result, urban governments will play an increasingly important role in providing emergency responses and overcoming the challenge of integrating refugees into local communities. Municipalities, as primary recipients of refugees and asylum seekers, will need to build the necessary infrastructure and housing to incorporate them. They will also need to develop new strategies and policies to help people from different cultures and socio-economic backgrounds integrate.

Policies, legislation and regulations

Change in people's behavior

BOX 9: Cities Accommodating Refugees

Since 2012, Europe has experienced an increasing flow of a significant number of asylum seekers and refugees. In 2015, Germany alone received around one million refugees (Katz, Noring, and Garrelts, 2016). Most of them have settled in Germany's big cities. As a result, local governments have had the responsibility to design and plan policies and initiatives rapidly in order to integrate the new arrivals. These actions include providing different urban services, such as housing, education, health care, language courses, job training and workforce integration, public safety and security, etc.

Leipzig

The German city of Leipzig, the largest city in the federal state of Saxony with a population of some 570,000 people, is one of the cities that have been working in the past few years to provide a response to the refugee crisis. According to the country's quota agreement, Saxony is required to take in 5.1% of all new refugees applying for asylum in Germany, of which 13% were then allocated to the city of Leipzig. As of September 2016, there were 4,434 asylum seekers living in Leipzig (City of Leipzig, 2016).

The municipality has designed and implemented a number of initiatives and programs to integrate refugees and asylum seekers. In addition to providing housing and other basic benefits such as healthcare and language courses, the city government has initiated additional actions so that social inclusion is sustainable in the long-term. For instance, the City of Leipzig has been organizing "Intercultural Weeks" to promote cultural and religious diversity; provided training on interculturality for employees within the city administration; and offered language and cultural translation services to municipal agencies (Eurocities, 2015). Additionally, in 2014 the municipality launched the "Arriving in Leipzig, Mentors for Refugees" project, so that citizens can voluntarily provide additional help to refugees. As of 2015, more than 1,000 citizens had signed up for the program and more than 300 mentorships had been created (Eurocities, 2015).

Hamburg

The city-state of Hamburg is another German city showing innovative approaches to designing arrival policies for newcomers and planning economic and social integration. As the second largest city in Germany with a population of some 1.7 million residents in the city and more than 5 million inhabitants in the Hamburg Metropolitan Region, it has received disproportionally more refugees per square kilometer than other German states. In terms of numbers of refugees received, it ranks after Berlin (first) and before Bremen (third), the two other city-states in the country (Katz et al., 2016) These city-states are also home to the most residents per square kilometer.

At the beginning of 2017, about 51,500 refugees lived in Hamburg, 8,300 of whom were in initial reception facilities (NDR, 2017). Hamburg spent some €586 million in 2015 and €900 million in 2016 on accommodating refugees and asylum seekers (Katz et al., 2016; NDR, 2017). This included costs for emergency reception, meals, transportation, healthcare, security and schooling.

Besides the provision of direct services, various initiatives were launched to successfully integrate refugees in the long-term. One of them is the **City-ScienceLab**, a collaboration between Hafencity University and the MIT Media Lab Changing Places Group. The main goal of the lab is to create a research unit to explore processes of urbanization in the digital age and deploy tangible-digital city models (Noyman, 2016). The models allow policymakers to discuss solutions for the thousands of refugees in Hamburg, including accommodation. They will also collaborate with universities, companies and local initiatives. The Lab will investigate how these theoretical ideas can be applied to Hamburg through different experiments.

One scheme within the Lab is **CityScope**, a scalable 3D-platform that facilitates evidence-based, data-driven processes for urban design and which allows new approaches to citizens' participation (HCU, 2016). CityScope paved the way for the launch of FindingPlaces.hamburg, an urban modelling platform aimed at identifying areas for refugee accommodation in Hamburg. As of 2016, the city had accommodated some 39,000 asylum seekers and sought to find accommodation for some additional 20,000 refugees. This cooperative project ran between May 26 and July 15, 2016, a period during which Hamburgers have been searching for public spaces for the construction of refugee shelters in numerous workshops on interactive city models, the so-called CityScopes. At the end of the numerous workshops, some 400 Hamburgers proposed around 161 spaces, of which the city is evaluating some 44 of them (FINDINGPLACES.hamburg, 2016). The aim of the project is to **promote citizens' participation and a citywide dialogue** regarding how to accommodate refugees.

Moreover, **civil society** has been crucial in the accommodation of refugees. One initiative is Hanseatic Help, which was created to provide clothing, shoes and hygiene articles for refugees in 2015. Another project was a permanent refugee center in Hamburg that, as of 2016, had 140 volunteers for 190 refugees, including children (Katz et al., 2016). The volunteers provide assistance to refugees such as employment mentoring, homework aid, language training, and assistance with visits to doctors.

These voluntary initiatives, led by civil society both in Leipzig and Hamburg shows that, despite anti-refugees and anti-immigration movements, many individuals are also willing to help these groups. Additionally, these examples reflect the central role that local authorities can play in successfully integrating refugees. However, they must also effectively coordinate with regional and national governments, as well as civil society and private partners.

Hamburg, Germany

Source: Pixabay, CC0

3.3.2 Inclusiveness of Senior Citizens in Society

With increasingly ageing societies in cities, it is essential to make sure that older people do not become isolated and continue to play a critical role in their communities. Through small actions and initiatives, city managers and planners can improve the quality of life of senior citizens and include them in the political, cultural and economic life of the city.

One particularly important area of action is the improvement of transportation and outdoor spaces. By improving public transport and the number of walking areas, older people can find it easier to move around the city, avoiding segregation and isolation. Another important area is healthcare and social inclusion. New technologies and innovations, such as sensors and digital applications in e-health and social care systems, can be crucial for improving the care and the quality of life of the elderly. Additionally, civic participation and community engagement is also very important.

Policies, legislation and regulations

New applied technologies and innovations

BOX 10: City Initiatives to Avoid Elderly Isolation and Improve their Participation in Society

The following three city initiatives were designed to increase senior citizen participation, reduce social exclusion and isolation, and improve their quality of life.

"Vincles" – Barcelona, Spain

In 2015, there were 300,000 elderly people living in Barcelona and one out of four citizens aged 65 or over lived alone (Ajuntament de Barcelona, 2016). To fight the emotional and social isolation faced by senior citizens in Barcelona, the city government launched the "Vincles" initiative. "Vincles" (translated as *bonds*) seeks to strengthen the social ties of elderly people in the city, reduce loneliness and improve quality of life with the help of new technologies.

The program provides a tablet with the user-friendly Vincles app, which has two platforms, to senior citizens. The platform connects the person's network of friends, family, neighbors and care givers to so they can chat and coordinate their activities. It also provides a social network that bonds older people with each other, enabling them to meet or chat online (Bloomberg Philantropies, 2016). The "Vincles" project won the first prize in the Bloomberg Philanthropies Mayors Challenge Europa 2014.

"FutureCity" Initiative – Yokohama, Japan

Japan has the highest population of people who are over 65 in the world. It is projected that by 2050, the proportion of people over 65 will make up 40% of the country's population (Japan For Sustainability, 2016). This demographic phenomenon is creating important challenges in many cities in Japan. To create and promote solutions for a variety of social and environmental issues, and to improve the quality of life for older people, the Japanese Government launched the "FutureCity" Initiative (FCI) in 2011. The FCI's goal is to create people-friendly cities that can overcome the challenges of ageing societies, as well as deal with environmental issues.

As of 2014, 11 cities were running the initiative. One of them is Yokohama, the second largest city in Japan with some 3.7 million people. Around 22% of the population is over 65 years old and, according to estimates, the number of senior citizens will reach approximately 1 million by 2025. In order to tackle challenges related to an ageing society, the City of Yokohama has implemented various actions and projects within the framework of the "FutureCity" initiative. For instance, the city government realized that a high percentage of the city's older population lived in the "new town districts" of the city, where they moved in the 1960s and 1970s. Many of these districts do not have adequate transportation, infrastructure and healthcare, all critical services for senior citizens. To improve the situation, the city invested in improving public transportation and healthcare services in these areas, specifically to meet the long-term challenges of demographic change.

A particularly successful program was the "Yokohama Walking Point Program," aimed at improving the health of citizens while reducing CO_2 emissions. The program encourages walking instead of taking the car by using a system of rewards (OECD, 2015). With this and other projects and regulations, the city has been able to transform some suburban parts of the city into lively urban areas, especially for older generations.

The City of Yokohama, Japan

"Cuidamos Pozuelo" – Pozuelo de Alarcón, Spain

In 2016, the City Council of Pozuelo de Alarcón, a municipality in the Community of Madrid in Spain, launched the "Cuidamos Pozuelo" initiative (translated as *we take care of Pozuelo*). A volunteer pilot project, it encourages the active participation of older people through collaboration in different municipal areas. A network of senior volunteers observes the city's environment and sends a weekly report to the City Council, providing information on the deterioration of infrastructure or the city's outdoor furniture. This includes details of problems with sidewalks, sewage systems or road signs, which can then be repaired.

The project improves public urban spaces, while actively promoting participation of the ageing population (Ayuntamiento de Pozuelo de Alarcón, 2016). In the first three months of the pilot project, July-September 2016, senior citizens sent a total of 190 notifications for needed improvements to the city.

***

3.3.3 Disabled People

People with disabilities face many obstacles in their daily life and they are often unable to access parts of the city. Using transportation systems or navigating public spaces in cities is sometimes difficult for people in wheelchairs or who are visually impaired. This limits their ability to participate in city life or find a job, placing them at a high risk of social exclusion. Local governments should implement programs and strategies that promote full accessibility for all citizens, including people with disabilities, through optimal design.

New applied technologies and innovations

BOX 11: Virtual Warsaw – Improving Accessibility for the Visually Impaired

Warsaw is the capital and the largest city in Poland with a population of around 1.7 million people in the city and some 3 million people in the greater metropolitan area. The city is a political, economic and cultural center, with a GDP per capita of some €26,100 (2013).

Some 40,000 visually impaired people live in the city of Warsaw. A survey found that more than 80% of visually impaired residents felt dependent on others in their daily activities, and it took them between 60 and 90 hours of training to be able to move freely in the city (Bloomberg Philantropies, 2016). Additionally, the unemployment rate among the city's blind population is around 80%.

To improve accessibility and inclusiveness of blind and visually impaired people, the local government decided to employ new technologies, specifically Internet of Things Technology (IoT). They developed the **Virtual Warsaw** app, which provides navigation prompts and easy access to key information such as bus times and opening hours, and installed thousands of beacons around the city that communicates directly with smartphones (Bloomberg Philantropies, 2016).

Through this innovation, the city of Warsaw aims to facilitate freer and more independent movement of the blind and visually impaired people around the city. The initiative helps them navigate public transportation, as well as locate public buildings and cultural locations. It also offers an individualized support system with training and career consultation services to help them enter the job market and connect with other visually impaired residents (OECD, 2017).

From 2014 to 2016, the technology was tested through different pilot programs in partnership with the Polish Association for the Blind and Visually Impaired. A private service provider, Ifinity, was designated as the technology provider and mobile app designer. The company worked in collaboration with the municipality during initial phase of the project. The app placed as a finalist in the Bloomberg Mayor Challenge in 2014, receiving $1.25 million in funding that was added to money coming from the European Union (Ifinity, 2015). In addition, in 2015 the Virtual Warsaw project was named the 2014 Golden Antenna of Telecommunications World for Product of the Year.

The city is currently expanding the Virtual Warsaw program with full implementation expected by 2021. The program will also include 24 other regional municipalities, encompassing a large number of connection points (OECD, 2017). There are plans to use the beacons for other purposes, such as for tourists or to measure air quality, thus increasing the potential impact of this initiative.

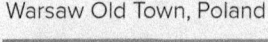

Warsaw Old Town, Poland

***

3.4 Safer and Healthier Cities for All

Safe and healthy urban spaces are essential for a good quality of life and well-being. High levels of violence and crime require effective coordination between city governments and local police. Along with police, local governments can take action on different levels to increase safety and security in cities. By **improving urban design** or by implementing **initiatives and strategies to encourage changes in people's behavior**, safer and healthier cities can be created.

3.4.1 Safety and Security

As mentioned in the volume *Cities and Mobility & Transportation* (Berrone, Ricart, and Duch T-Figueras, 2016), more than 1.2 million people die each year on the roads worldwide. Moreover, up to 50 million persons endure non-fatal injuries, with 50% of deaths and 75% of injuries occurring in urban areas. To solve this important issue of public safety and health, some cities have implemented strategies, programs and road-safety plans to lower the number of accidents and achieve traffic safety in urban areas.

Change in people's behavior and preferences

Policies, legislation and regulations

BEST PRACTICE: LA PAZ
— Zebras for Traffic Safety and Youth Empowerment

La Paz is the administrative capital of Bolivia (the constitutional capital is Sucre) and the third most populous city with a population of almost 800,000 city dwellers. The metropolitan area is the most populous in the country, with almost 2 million people. At an elevation of some 3,650 meters above sea level, it is the highest capital in the world. The city is an important political, economic and cultural

La Paz, Bolivia

Photo: Ana Duch

center. In 2014, La Paz Department contributed more than 25% of the nation's GDP (INE, 2016).

Context

- Many cities in Latin America are designed for the movement of cars rather than for pedestrians.

- Many people die or endure non-fatal injuries from traffic accidents every year in urban areas.

- La Paz and its metropolitan area have experienced an important population increase in recent decades, as people move from rural areas to urban areas.

- As population increases, so does the number of cars in the streets of the city.

- In La Paz, most drivers do not respect red traffic lights, and much less the right of pedestrians to cross the streets.

Actions

- To solve the problem and create a more sustainable urban mobility system, the City of La Paz launched the **Zebras' project**. The program was inspired by one created by the city of Bogota, Colombia.

- Kicked off by the La Paz Government in 2001, the program features people dressed in zebra costumes, known as *cebritas*, who **direct traffic and make sure that pedestrians can cross the streets safely**. The *cebritas* move, jump, yell and wave flags in a fun way to get the attention of pedestrians and car-drivers.

- The initiative aims to **transform people's behavior through an educational traffic safety network focused on pedestrians and car-drivers**. The program seeks to change negative behaviors such as not respecting pedestrian crossings, ignoring traffic lights, etc.

- The program also aims to help poor and vulnerable youth. Most of the *cebritas* are young people from disadvantaged backgrounds. The City Government hires them as urban educators on a part-time basis, paying them minimum wage.

- The program initially included only 24 *cebritas*.

Outcomes

- After more than a decade, the program has been a success: local drivers are significantly more cautious than before; the number of traffic accidents decreased; the quality of pedestrian spaces improved; and vulnerable youth at risk of social exclusion benefitted in a tangible way.

- As of 2017, the project has some 300 *cebritas* and has been replicated to other cities of Bolivia, such as El Alto, Sucre, Oruro or Tarija (Henderson, 2017; Secretariat of Guangzhou International Award for Urban Innovation, 2016).

- More than 3,000 youth have been part of the project in recent years, helping them avoid delinquency, while becoming actively involved in a citizen education program (Secretariat of Guangzhou International Award for Urban Innovation, 2016).

- The initiative accomplished various goals simultaneously: it **improved citizens' behavior** while **increasing safety in the city**, and also **advanced social inclusion by helping vulnerable youth reduce their risk of social exclusion and poverty**.

- In 2015, UNESCO declared the La Paz Zebras a "cultural asset" for their role in strengthening civic culture.

Cebritas in Sucre

Photo: Ana Duch

- In 2016, the Zebras project won the Guangzhou International Award for Urban Innovation.

As previously mentioned, urban planning and design play an intrinsic role in improving safety and security in cities. Appropriate urban lighting, ongoing maintenance of public spaces and a safe mobility network can reduce the risk of violence in urban spaces, for instance.

| Policies, legislation and regulations | Infrastructure and urban planning | New applied technologies and innovations |

BOX 12: Safe Urban Spaces for Women for Equal Opportunities

Inclusive and equitable cities require the full participation of women in all areas of society. Yet, **women often face a higher risk of experiencing violence or ha-rassment in cities than men**. This, consequently, diminishes their opportunities for participation in city activities. To alter this situation and move toward gender equality, actions in specific areas are needed. City governments should engage in dialogue with women and take into account their views, needs and opinions when designing public spaces and urban infrastructures.

Local governments can work to eliminate the exclusion and discrimination of women through targeted training and skills development, specific financial in-struments or positive discrimination policies (such as a minimum quota of women in local government positions). They can also improve the participation of girls and women in urban life by providing safe environments, where they can move, work and enjoy public spaces. This can be achieved through simple actions such as improving urban lighting systems or sidewalks, and/or ensuring laws against sexual harassment and violence.

Vienna – Gender Mainstreaming

Vienna was one of the first cities in the world to include gender issues in their ur-ban planning and urban agenda. Since the late 1990s, the Austrian capital start-ed to include equality measures in city planning. One of the first actions taken by the City Administration was to ask women about their mobility patterns in the city. It discovered that these were different than those of men, with women more fre-quently using public transportation and going to places on foot (Foran, 2013). As a result, city planners decided to alter the city's planning by improving the public transportation system, widening sidewalks, adding extra ramps for strollers, and upgrading street lighting so women could feel safer walking at night.

Taking into account a gender point of view when defining public policy is a strategy that the City of Vienna calls "**gender mainstreaming**." The final goal of the strategy is foment a gender-sensitive society and offer equal opportunities to women by providing equal access to the city. Since the first initiative, the local administration has applied a gender mainstreaming vision to projects and initiatives in many different areas of city management, such as work and education, culture and leisure, and public space. UN-Habitat included Vienna's Gender Mainstreaming Strategy in its archive of best practices to improve equality in cities (UN-Habitat, 2008). As part of its efforts to continue working toward gender equality, in 2009 the City also introduced the Equality Action Plan, a full package of activities and initiatives aimed at securing a gender perspective (Vienna City Administration, n.d.).

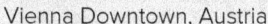

Vienna Downtown, Austria

Tracking sexual harassment – The cases of Cairo and Beirut

More than 95% of women in Cairo have suffered some form of sexual harassment in the streets of the Egyptian capital. To find a solution to this problem and create a safe environment for people of all genders, HarrasMap, a **bottom-up volunteer-based initiative**, started in 2010. HarrasMap is a website created to track and document harassment. Anonymous SMS and online reporting of sexual harassment and assault is uploaded to an online map. The final goal of the initiative is two-fold. First, incidents are documented and tracked so that pressure can be applied to local governments to take action either through policy or by specific actions, such as improving lighting and sidewalks to improve safety for women. The second goal is to create a public debate and raise awareness in society that sexual harassment cannot be tolerated.

Following this initiative, activists from more than 25 countries launched similar initiatives. For instance, at the beginning of 2016 in Beirut (Lebanon), a similar online reporting tool for sexual harassment was created, Harasstracker. The tool can be used not only for street harassment, but also for harassment in private places, such as homes, schools, shops and work spaces. It also provides information for the victims on what to do and offers them help. The final goal of the initiative is similar to the previous one: it aims to raise awareness of the issue and offer information. Furthermore, it seeks to influence public policy and encourage the creation of new laws to protect women against sexual harassment. These initiatives face a hurdle, however. Although the tools are easy to use, not all citizens – especially older people – know how to use the Internet and digital applications.

**

3.4.2 Healthy Populations

Lastly, healthy populations are essential for achieving equitable and socially inclusive cities that offer a high quality of life and well-being for inhabitants.

New applied technologies and innovations

BOX 13: Clean Lahore: Fighting Dengue with Technology

Dengue fever is a mosquito-borne disease that produces fever and pain. In 2011, there was an outbreak of dengue fever in the region of Punjab, Pakistan. It was the worst dengue epidemics in the regions' history. Just in Lahore, which is the capital of the province of Punjab and the second largest city in Pakistan, more than 21,000 cases of dengue fever were reported (Bhatti, Kusek, and Verheijen, 2015). This was a serious public health issue, since almost every household in the city was affected. But it was also an economic and political crisis because Lahore is a major economic, cultural and historic center in the country.

The government asked Dr. Umar Saif, the new chairman of the Punjab Information Technology Board (PITB) to identify a solution (Bhatti et al., 2015).

He realized that there was a lack of data on where new infections were occurring. The PITB developed a smartphone application, the **Clean Lahore app**. The goal of the app was to help stop the spread of the illness by recording and geo-tracking where new cases were emerging with pictures. Photos were pinned to a map of Lahore (http://www.dashboard.tracking.punjab.gov. pk), along with data about patients and larvae, which were systematically analyzed. With this data, the government and the health department could focus preventive activities on those areas of the city that were most affected. They could also clear out large pools of standing water, where mosquitoes that carries the disease puts larvae. This, in turn, would help curtail major outbreaks. In 2012, only 258 cases of dengue were diagnosed – 80 times fewer cases than in 2011.

This is an innovative example of how cities can collect data through mobile phones, which are relatively inexpensive, to make major improvements in public health.

Infrastructure and urban planning

Change in people's behavior and preferences

BEST PRACTICE: OKLAHOMA CITY
— Promoting Collective Health

Oklahoma City is a medium size city in the USA and the capital and largest city in the State of Oklahoma with a population of some 630,000 inhabitants in the city and around 1.3 million people in the metropolitan area. Its main industries are technology and energy, with oil, natural gas, petroleum and related industries being

Oklahoma City, USA

Source: Pixabay, CC0

the largest economic sector of the local economy. Additionally, the city is one of the main travel corridors into Texas and Mexico. The gross metropolitan product is US$67.7 billion and the median household income of above $US 50,000 (OKCPD, n.d.).

Context

- Obesity is one of the most important health issues in the U.S. This problem is particularly acute in Oklahoma, where almost one third of adults are obese, one in five children aged 10-17 suffers obesity, and nearly one third of pre-school infants are overweight (Birrell, 2015).

- Oklahoma City is one of the most spread-out cities in the U.S., covering 620 square miles, with some 600,000 residents relying on cars. In the early 2000s, it did not have a single bike line in the entire city.

- Additionally, the diet of Oklahoma's residents wasn't very healthy. In fact, the city had one of the highest density of fast-food restaurants in the USA, with 40 McDonald's and other fast foods restaurant chains in operation (Birrell, 2015). Health-food stores were few and spread out. Furthermore, the state ranked among the worst in fruit and vegetable consumption (DeHority, n.d.).

- In 2007, *Men's Fitness* called Oklahoma "the 8th fattest city" in America.

- In 2008, Oklahoma City was ranked "the worst walking city" in the USA in a study by Prevention magazine and the American Podiatric Medical Association (APMA).

Actions

- After reading in 2007 that Oklahoma was one of the fattest cities in the U.S. and realizing that he himself was obese, Mick Cornett – who had been mayor since 2004 – decided to take action. Many health issues, in particular of obesity, are linked with specific behaviors. Cornett sought to improve citizens' health by trying to change their behavior.

- Cornett challenged his citizens to "collectively lose a million pounds." To achieve this goal, a website called "This City is Going on a Diet" was created to provide a platform with healthy diet tips, the location of public parks and answer questions regarding obesity (DeHority, n.d.). The program was a success and in January 2012, the city reached the goal of losing 1 million pounds with some 47,000 people signed up in the program, losing on average 20 pounds each. It constituted a massive public awareness campaign, with citizens, business and the government all involved.

- In addition to the initiative, the city also started programs and urban planning policies in other areas to change behaviors, redesign the city to make it more walkable and keep its citizens active and healthy. These included building health facilities in low-income neighborhoods, increasing health education in the schools, making sure there are gyms in all grade schools and building public urban infrastructures (CityofOKC, 2016).

- In 2009, the mayor led the campaign to approve the so-called "MAPS-3" program, a $777 million sales tax issue to fund projects focused on health, infrastructures for walkability and quality of life, and economic development. (America Walks, 2014).

- The "MAPS- 3" program started in 2010 and will last until 2021. It includes different projects such as a 70-acre Downtown Public Park, to inspire communities to spend time outside and promote healthier lifestyles; public transit improvements; sports facilities; and additional bike trails and sidewalks for walking, cycling and running. Also featured in the plan are senior health and wellness centers that encourage healthier and more active lifestyles, and which will serve as gathering places for seniors - thus reducing the risk of isolation of this growing group in society.

- Additionally, $140 million of Tax Increment Financing funds were used to redesign and rebuild the city downtown to increase walkability: from narrowing roadways, to widening sidewalks, and adding trees in the streets (America Walks, 2014).

Outcomes

- This is a good example of how a mayor's vision on health and wellness can change people's behavior towards healthier ways of living, improving people's quality of life.

- Additionally, it also shows how urban design and infrastructure can have an important effect on people's behaviors and preferences. The city had been planned around cars instead of people. To solve this problem, hundreds of miles of new bike trails and sidewalks were constructed. Additionally, the city downtown is being rebuilt with the construction of parks and public spaces towards a more walkable city.

- The city still ranks in the lower 15% of cities in the USA in terms of walkability, but it has improved from previous rankings (Walljasper, n.d.). It is expected to continue improving as more sidewalks and trails are being built.

- In the lowest-income areas of the city, where there are the highest rates of diabetes and blood-pressure problems, key statistics have been cut by between 2% and 10% in five years (Birrell, 2015). Additionally, the mortality rates have decreased by 3%.

- Lastly, despite the fact that Oklahoma's obesity rate is still increasing, it has slowed down significantly from 6% a year to 1% (Walljasper, n.d.).

- In 2012, the city was among the fittest of the abovementioned *Men's Fitness* magazine.

- Its local city county health department has become a national model and has been considered a "laboratory for healthy living."

- Ultimately, the strategy has not only had a positive effect on people's health, but it has also helped economic development in Oklahoma City. It has helped the city attract businesses and high-educated young Millennials who want to live in a city offering a high quality of life.

***

4. Concluding Remarks

Urban inclusion is a multi-faceted issue, covering social, spatial, economic and security dimensions. Challenges of segregation, poverty, increasing inequalities, lack of access to key services (such as education, health, water and sanitation, energy or waste management) and concerns of public order and security are on the rise in cities around the world. To create socially cohesive cities, local leaders need to take **an integrated, holistic approach** to deal with all of the abovementioned dimensions and challenges.

A socially cohesive city is not one where everyone is equal, but one where everyone has **equal opportunities of access and participation** (with no discrimination and marginalization); that offers **social mobility** (with reductions of inequality and poverty); and where there is **tolerance and respect for diversity and identification**. Municipal governments play a key role in achieving this goal. First, cities are better positioned to communicate with citizens and to understand their most pressing social issues and needs. Second, they provide most of the basic services and infrastructures to ensure equal opportunities and avoid poverty traps. And third, they hold the key to fostering cooperation among diverse stakeholders and levels of government (regional and national).

City authorities must seek and adopt strategies and competencies that **put citizens' needs back at the center of policies**. To find sustainable solutions to the complex challenges of social cohesion, local governments should implement integrated initiatives and strategies, and cooperate on local, regional, national and international levels. They should work closely with all stakeholders in the private sector, public sector (e.g. educational and health institutions and the police), as well as with educational institutions, NGOs and civil society.

Cities have different sizes, development levels, demographic and social contexts, as well as cultural and economic realities. Local governments need to define strategies and policies that take into account the diversity of their cities, and leverage it as a source of new opportunities and socio-economic development, rather than see it as a problem. In this volume, we have described different initiatives, strategies, programs and models in cities around the world to overcome problems of social exclusion and marginalization, while creating a better quality of life for citizens.

We have seen the need to provide: **basic urban services and infrastructures** to avoid social exclusion, poverty and spatial segregation; **affordable housing** for all, with access to basic facilities such as water and sanitation, energy, waste management and accessibility to public transport, which are crucial to overcome poverty and inequality; **quality education and health**; improved **access to credit and finances**, which can significantly increase job opportunities and employment prospects; and lastly, innovative solutions and strategies to foster the **integration of diverse communities and ethnicities**. By accelerating progress in these areas, it will be possible to create **more cohesive, safer and healthier cities, while improving people's quality of life and well-being.**

5. References

Ajuntament de Barcelona (2016). VinclesBCN. Retrieved from http://ajuntament. barcelona.cat/vinclesbcn/en/

Albert, P. J., Werhane, P., and Rolph, T. (2014). Global Poverty Alleviation: A Case Book. *The International Society of Business, Economics, and Ethics Book Series, 3.*

America Walks (2014). *Oklahoma City Case Study.*

Atuesta, L. H., and Soares, Y. (2016). Urban Upgrading in Rio de Janeiro: Evidence from the Favela-Bairro programme. *Urban Studies*, 1–18.

Ayuntamiento de Pozuelo de Alarcón (2016). Cuidemos Pozuelo. *Vive Pozuelo - Num. 141.*

Berrone, P., Ricart, J. E., and Duch T-Figueras, A. I. (2016). *Cities and Mobility & Transportation: Towards the Next Generation of Urban Mobility.* CreateSpace.

Berrone, P., Ricart, J. E., and Duch T-Figueras, A. I. (2017). *Cities and the Economy: Fueling Growth, Jobs and Innovation.* CreateSpace.

Bhatti, Z. K., Kusek, J. Z., and Verheijen, T. (2015). *Logged On: Smart Government Solutions from South Asia.* Washington DC: World Bank.

Birrell, I. (2015). America's most overweight cities: How Oklahoma is battling obesity. *The Independent.* Retrieved from http://www.independent.co.uk/life-style/ health-and-families/features/americas-most-overweight-cities-how-oklahoma-is-battling-obesity-a6721901.html

Blom, S. (2014). *Local Migration and Integration Policies in Amsterdam - KING Project.* Milano: Fondazione ISMU - Iniziative e Studi sulla Multietnicità.

Bloomberg Philanthropies (2016). *Bringing Bold Ideas to Life: Insights from Innovators Taking Part in Bloomberg Philanthropies' Mayors Challenge.*

C40 (2013). Rio de Janeiro: Morar Carioca. Retrieved March 24, 2017, from http://www.c40.org/profiles/2013-riodejaneiro

Catalytic Communities (2015). Rio Favela Facts. Retrieved March 23, 2017, from http://catcomm.org/favela-facts/

CBS (2017). StatLine database - Centraal Bureau voor de Statistiek. Retrieved March 16, 2017, from http://statline.cbs.nl/StatWeb/publication/?VW=T&DM=SLNL&PA=70748NED&D1=0,2,4,16,18,20,22,24&D2=a&D3=0&D4=a&D5=l&HD=090707-1905&HDR=T&STB=G4,G2,G1,G3

City of Leipzig (2016). Refugees in Leipzig. Retrieved March 31, 2017, from http://english.leipzig.de/youth-family-and-community/foreign-nationals-and-migrants/refugees-in-leipzig/

City of New York (2016). Mandatory Inclusionary Housing. Retrieved March 31, 2017, from http://www1.nyc.gov/site/planning/plans/mih/mandatory-inclusionary-housing.page

CityofOKC (2016). *Oklahoma City Mayor Mick Cornett's 2016 State of the City Address - YouTube*. Retrieved from https://www.youtube.com/watch?v=NLcuNBvnD9E

Coalition for Smarter Growth (2016). DC Inclusionary Zoning. Retrieved March 31, 2017, from http://www.smartergrowth.net/IZ/

DeHority, S. (n.d.) Success Story: Oklahoma City Drops 1 Million Pounds. *Men's Fitness*. Retrieved from http://www.mensfitness.com/weight-loss/success-stories/success-story-oklahoma-city-drops-1-million-pounds

EUKN (2014). *The Inclusive City: Approaches to Combat Urban Poverty and Social Exclusion in Europe* (Report). The Hague: European Urban Knowledge Network EGTC.

Eurocities (2015). Cities welcome refugees - Leipzig. Retrieved March 31, 2017, from http://www.eurocities.eu/eurocities/events/Cities-welcome-refugees-Leipzig-WSPO-A33EYC

Euromonitor International (2017). Passport Database - Cities.

European Union (2011). *Cities of Tomorrow: Challenges, Visions, Ways Forward*. Brussels: European Commission, Directorate General for Regional Policy.

FAO (2015). The State of Food Insecurity in the World 2015. Retrieved March 30, 2017, from http://www.fao.org/hunger/key-messages/en/

FINDINGPLACES.hamburg (2016). Mitreden. Mitsuchen. Erfahren Sie, was FindingPlaces ist. Retrieved April 6, 2017, from https://www.findingplaces. hamburg/

Foran, C. (2013). How to Design a City for Women - CityLab. Retrieved February 24, 2017, from http://www.citylab.com/commute/2013/09/how-design-city-women/6739/

Gemeente Amsterdam (2016). *Amsterdamse Burgermonitor 2015: Onderzoek, Informatie en Statistiek.*

Harvey, D. (2003). The Right to the City. *International Journal of Urban and Regional Research, 27*(4), 939–941.

HCU (2016). CityScienceLab - HafenCity Universität Hamburg. Retrieved April 6, 2017, from https://www.hcu-hamburg.de/research/citysciencelab/

Henderson, I. (2017). Big in Bolivia: Zebra in the Streets. *The Atlantic.* Retrieved from https://www.theatlantic.com/magazine/archive/2017/03/zebras-in-the-streets/513836/

Herrine, L., Yager, J., and Mian, N. (2016). *Gentrification Response: A Survey of Strategies to Maintain Neighborhood Economic Diversity.* NYU Furman Center.

Iamsterdam (2016). Amsterdam Facts and Figures. Retrieved March 15, 2017, from http://www.iamsterdam.com/en/visiting/about-amsterdam/facts-and-figures

Iamsterdam (2017). Diversity in Amsterdam. Retrieved January 25, 2017, from http://www.iamsterdam.com/en/local/about-amsterdam/people-culture/diversity-in-the-city

IDB (2011). *Development Effectiveness Overview.* New York: Inter-American Development Bank.

Ifinity (2015). Virtual Warsaw will be worth $15 million. Retrieved March 22, 2017, from http://getifinity.com/virtual-warsaw-will-be-worth-15-million/

ILO (2016). *World Employment Social Outlook 2016: Trends for Youth.* International Labour Organization.

INE (2016). Instituto Nacional de Estadística: Producto Interno Bruto Departamental. Retrieved February 24, 2017, from http://www.ine.gob.bo/indice/general. aspx?codigo=40203

INSEE (2016a). Étrangers - Immigrés en 2013 - Département de Paris. Retrieved February 13, 2017, from https://www.insee.fr/fr/statistiques/2020940?sommaire= 2106113&geo=DEP-75

INSEE (2016b). La localisation géographique des immigrés: Une forte concentration dans l'aire urbaine de Paris. *Insee Première nº1591*.

IOM (2015a). *Global Migration Trends 2015 Factsheet*. Berlin: Global Migration Data Analysis Centre International Organization for Migration.

IOM (2015b). *World Migration Report 2015*. Geneva: International Organization for Migration.

IWA (2016). Cities of the Future - International Water Association. Retrieved March 21, 2017, from http://www.iwa-network.org/programs/cities-of-the-future/

Japan For Sustainability (2016). "FutureCity" Initiative. Retrieved from http://www.japanfs.org/en/projects/future_city/index.html

Katz, B., Noring, L., and Garrelts, N. (2016). *Cities and Refugees – The German Experience*. Washington, DC: Brookings Centennial Scholar Initiative.

Kearns, A., and Forrest, R. (2000). Social cohesion and multilevel urban governance. *Urban Studies, 37*(5–6), 995–1017. Journal Article.

Luccl, P., Bhatkal, T., Khan, A., and Berliner, T. (2015). *What works in improving the living conditions of slum dwellers*. London: Overseas Development Institute.

Magalhães, F., and di Villarosa, F. (2012). *Slum Upgrading – Lessons Learned from Brazil*. Washington, D.C.: Inter-American Development Bank.

Matheson, R. (2016). Study: Mobile-money Services Lift Kenyans Out of Poverty - MIT News. Retrieved March 29, 2017, from http://news.mit.edu/2016/mobile-money-kenyans-out-poverty-1208

Moloney, T., and Kirchberger, A. (2010). *Cities Accomodating Diversity: Findings and Recommendations from the Peer Review Project "Diversity and Equality in European Cities."* EUROCITIES.

Muthiora, B. (2015). *Enabling Mobile Money Policies in Kenya: Fostering a Digital Financial Revolution*. GSMA's Mobile Money for the Unbanked.

NDR (2017). CDU kritisiert Flüchtlingskosten in Hamburg. Retrieved April 6, 2017, from http://www.ndr.de/nachrichten/hamburg/CDU-kritisiert-Fluechtlingskosten-in-Hamburg,fluechtlinge6610.html

Noyman, A. (2016). Urban Modelling for Refugees in Hamburg. Retrieved April 6, 2017, from http://cp.media.mit.edu/blog/47jn7w5659tdzh9jefrahnf38khk5m

Numbeo (2016). Property Prices. Retrieved from https://www.numbeo.com/property-investment/

Numbeo (2017). Crime Index by City 2017. Retrieved January 17, 2017, from https://www.numbeo.com/crime/rankings.jsp

OECD (2015). *Ageing in Cities: Policy Highlights*. Paris: OECD Publishing.

OECD (2017). Case Study: Virtual Warsaw. Retrieved from https://www.oecd.org/gov/innovative-government/embracing-innovation-in-government-poland.pdf

OKCPD (n.d.) City of OKC : Why Choose Oklahoma City? - Oklahoma City Police Department. Retrieved March 22, 2017, from https://www.okc.gov/departments/police/recruiting/why-choose-oklahoma-city

OLIO (2016). The Problem of Food Waste - OLIO. Retrieved March 30, 2017, from https://olioex.com/food-waste/the-problem-of-food-waste/

Osborn, C. (2012). A History of Favela Upgrades Part II: Introducing Favela-Bairro (1988-2008) - RioOnWatch. Retrieved March 28, 2017, from http://www.rioonwatch.org/?p=5931

Oxford Poverty, and Human Development Initiative (2016). *Global Multidimensional Poverty Index Databank*. OPHI, University of Oxford.

Safaricom Limited (2017). Celebrating 10 Years of Changing Lives. Retrieved March 29, 2017, from http://www.safaricom.co.ke/mpesa_timeline/timeline.html

Salgado de Snyder, V. N., Friel, S., Fotso, J. C., Khadr, Z., Meresman, S., Monge, P., and Patil-Deshmukh, A. (2011). Social conditions and urban health inequities: realities, challenges and opportunities to transform the urban landscape through research and action. *Journal of Urban Health : Bulletin of the New York Academy of Medicine, 88*(6), 1183–93.

Secretaria Municipal de Habitação (n.d.) Favela-Bairro. Retrieved March 24, 2017, from http://www0.rio.rj.gov.br/habitacao/favela_bairro.htm

Secretaria Municipal do Habitat (n.d.) Minha Casa Minha Vida no Rio. Retrieved March 24, 2017, from http://www0.rio.rj.gov.br/habitacao/minha_casa_minha_vida.htm

Secretariat of Guangzhou International Award for Urban Innovation (2016). The La Paz Zebras: Citizen culture project. Retrieved February 24, 2017, from http://www.urban-innovations.org/index.php/The_La_Paz_Zebras:_Citizen_culture_project

Skoll (2015). Ciudad Saludable. Retrieved April 6, 2017, from http://skoll.org/organization/ciudad-saludable/

Stromberg, B., and Sturtevant, L. (2016). *What Makes Inclusionary Zoning Happen?* Inclusionary Housing: A Series of Research & Policy Briefs - National Housing Conference.

The Economist Intelligence Unit (2015). *The Safe Cities Index 2015.*

UCLG (2015). *The Role of Local Governments in Promoting Gender Equality for Sustainability.*

UN (2015). *World Population Ageing.* United Nations Department of Economic and Social Affairs - Population Division.

UNECE (2006). *Ministerial Declaration on Social and Economic Challenges in Distressed Urban Areas in the Unece Region.*

UN-Habitat (2008). *Gender Mainstreaming in Local Authorities Best Practices.* Nairobi: United Nations Human Settlements Programme (UN-HABITAT).

UN-Habitat (2016a). Housing and slum upgrading. Retrieved from http://unhabitat. org/urban-themes/housing-slum-upgrading/

UN-Habitat (2016b). *Urbanization and Development: Emerging Futures. World Cities Report 2016.* Nairobi: United Nations Human Settlements Programme (UN-HABITAT).

UN-Habitat, and International City Leaders (2016). *2015 Global City Report.*

UNHCR (2017). Urban Refugees. Retrieved March 31, 2017, from http://www.unhcr. org/urban-refugees.html

United Nations Statistics Division (2016). UNdata database - Sustainable Development Goals Indicators. Retrieved from http://data.un.org/

van Heelsum, A. (2008). *Case Study on Diversity Policy in Employment and Service Provision in Amsterdam, the Netherlands.* Dublin: European Foundation for the Improvement of Living and Working Conditions.

Vienna City Administration (n.d.). Equality Action Plan for Vienna 2009-2012.

Walljasper, J. (n.d.). America's "Worst Walking City" Gets Back on its Feet | AmericaWalks. Retrieved March 22, 2017, from http://americawalks.org/ americas-worst-walking-city-gets-back-on-its-feet/

WEF (2017). *Harnessing Public-Private Cooperation to Deliver the New Urban Agenda.* Geneva: World Economic Forum.

WHO (2015). *Key Facts from JMP 2015 Report.* Geneva: World Health Organization.

WHO/UNICEF (2015). *Progress on Sanitation and Drinking Water – 2015 update and MDG assessment.* Geneva: UNICEF and World Health Organization 2015.

World Bank (2016a). Ending Extreme Poverty. Retrieved February 1, 2017, from http://www.worldbank.org/en/news/feature/2016/06/08/ending-extreme-poverty

World Bank (2016b). Energy Overview. Retrieved March 9, 2017, from http://www.worldbank.org/en/topic/energy/overview#1

World Bank (2017). World Bank Open Data. Retrieved from http://data.worldbank.org/

Youthful Cities (2016). *Global Urban Millennial Survey 2016.*

6. Appendix I: Additional Resources

On the IESE Cities in Motion Strategies website you will find additional related material and resources. Check the following links regularly to access our latest publications:

• IESE Cities in Motion Strategies: http://www.iese.edu/cim.

Additionally, the authors recommend the following Internet resources for more information on the topic:

• Cities Alliance: http://www.citiesalliance.org.
• Divercities: https://www.urbandivercities.eu.
• EAPN – European Anti-Poverty Network: http://www.eapn.eu.
• EUROCITIES: http://www.eurocities.eu.
• European Forum for Urban Security: https://efus.eu.
• ENSA – European Network of Social Authorities: http://www.ensa-network.eu.
• ESN – European Social Network: http://www.esn-eu.org.
• Global Cities Business Alliance: https://www.businessincities.com.
• Habitat III – The New Urban Agenda: https://habitat3.org.
• Leading Cities: http://leadingcities.org.
• Metropolis: http://www.metropolis.org.
• New Cities Foundation: http://www.newcitiesfoundation.org.

- OECD – Urban Development: http://www.oecd.org/regional/regional-policy/urbandevelopment.htm.
- PPPs for Cities: http://www.pppcities.org.
- Slum Dwellers International (SDI): http://knowyourcity.info.
- UN-Habitat: http://unhabitat.org.
- UN-Data: http://data.un.org.
- United Cities and Local Governments (UCLG): https://www.uclg.org.
- United Nations Statistics Division (UNstats): http://unstats.un.org.
- UN Women: http://www.unwomen.org.
- URBACT: http://urbact.eu.
- Womenability: http://www.womenability.org.
- World Bank: http://www.worldbank.org.
- World Health Organization (WHO): http://www.who.int.
- World Resources Institute (WRI): http://www.wri.org.
- Youthful Cities: http://www.youthfulcities.com.

7. Appendix II: Cities in Motion Index— Social Cohesion Dimension

This appendix includes a brief presentation of the IESE Cities in Motion Index, focusing on the social cohesion dimension. For more information on the index, please check the IESE Cities in Motion website www.iese.edu/cim, with all our latest publications.

CITIES IN MOTION INDEX

The Cities in Motion Index (*CIMI*) has been designed with the aim of constructing a "breakthrough" indicator in terms of its completeness, characteristics, comparability and the quality and objectivity of its information. Its goal is to enable measurement of the future sustainability of the world's main cities, as well as the quality of life of their inhabitants.

The *CIMI* aims to help the public and governments to understand the performance of 10 fundamental dimensions for a city: governance, urban planning, public management, technology, the environment, international outreach, social cohesion, mobility and transportation, human capital, and the economy. Thanks to its broad and integrated vision of the city, the

Cities in Motion Index enables to recognize the strengths and weaknesses of each city, allowing the identification of effective solutions.

The 2016 edition is the third consecutive **CIMI**, covering the years 2013, 2014 and 2015. It includes a total of 181 cities, of which 72 are capitals representing more than 80 different countries, as well as 77 indicators measuring the 10 relevant dimensions.

RANKING *CIMI* 2015

New York City (United States) is in first place in the overall ranking, driven by its performance in the dimensions of the economy (first place), technology (third place) and in human capital, public management, governance, international outreach, and mobility and transportation (fourth place). However, for another year, it continues to be in very low positions in the dimensions of social cohesion (position 161) and in environment (position 93). Following New York, we find London (UK) in the second place of the ranking and Paris (France) in the third place.

Of the 10 top positions of the ranking, four cities are in the U.S. (New York, San Francisco, Boston and Chicago); four cities are in Europe (London, Paris, Amsterdam and Geneva); one is in Asia (Seoul) and one in Oceania (Sydney).

TABLE A1. CITY RANKING. TOP 10

CIMI 2015	City (Country)
1	New York City (United States)
2	London (United Kingdom)
3	Paris (France)
4	San Francisco (United States)
5	Boston (United States)

6	Amsterdam (Netherlands)
7	Chicago (United States)
8	Seoul (South Korea)
9	Geneva (Switzerland)
10	Sydney (Australia)

DIMENSION: SOCIAL COHESION

Social cohesion is a sociological dimension of cities defined as the degree of consensus among the members of a social group or the perception of belonging to a common situation or project. It is a measure of the intensity of social interaction within the group. Social cohesion in the urban context refers to the degree of coexistence among groups of people with different incomes, cultures, ages and professions who live in a city. Concern about the city's social setting requires an analysis of factors such as immigration, community development, care of the elderly, the effectiveness of the health system and public inclusion and safety.

The presence of various groups in the same space and mixing and interaction between groups are essential in a sustainable urban system. In this context, social cohesion is a state in which there is a vision shared by citizens and the government of a model of society based on social justice, the primacy of the rule of law and solidarity. This allows us to understand the importance of policies that underpin social cohesion based on democratic values.

Table A2 sets out the indicators selected for this dimension, descriptions of them, their units of measurement, and the information sources. This selection of indicators seeks to incorporate all the sociological subdimensions of social cohesion, based on the different variables available.

TABLE A2. SOCIAL COHESION INDICATORS

Indicator	Description / Unit of measurement	Source
Ratio of deaths	Ratio of death per 100,000 inhabitants	Euromonitor
Crime rate	Crime rate	Numbeo
Health index	Health index	Numbeo
Unemployment rate	Unemployment rate (number of unemployed / labor force)	Euromonitor
Gini index	The Gini index varies from 0 to 100, with 0 being a situation of perfect	Euromonitor
Price of property	Price of property as percentage of income	Numbeo
Ratio of women workers	Ratio of women workers in the public administration	International Labor Organization

The ratio of deaths per 100,000 inhabitants and the crime rate are incorporated with a negative sign, while the health index is incorporated with a positive sign in the creation of this dimension's indicator. Employment, meanwhile, is a fundamental aspect in societies, to the extent that, according to historical evidence, a lack of employment can break the consensus or the implicit social contract. For this reason, the unemployment rate is incorporated with a negative sign in the dimension of social cohesion. However, the ratio of women workers in the public administration is incorporated with a positive sign, since it is an indicator of gender equality in access to government jobs.

The Gini index is calculated from the Gini coefficient and measures social inequality. It assumes a value equal to zero for situations in which there is a perfectly equitable income distribution (everyone has the same income) and it assumes the value equal to 100 when the income distribution is perfectly inequitable (one person has all the income and the others none). This indicator is incorporated into the dimension with a negative sign, since a higher index value has a negative effect on a city's social cohesion. Finally, the price of property as a percentage of income is also related negatively since, when the percentage of income to be used to buy a property increases, the incentives to belong to a particular city's society decrease.

RANKING – SOCIAL COHESION DIMENSION

Helsinki (Finland) is the city with the highest rating in the social cohesion dimension. It is a city with a low unemployment rate, an equitable distribution of income and the highest percentage of women in government positions (more than 70%). It is worth noting that eight of the top 10 cities in this ranking are European.

TABLE A3. RANKING BY DIMENSION: SOCIAL COHESION

City, Country	Social Cohesion Ranking	CIMI 2015 Ranking
Helsinki, Finland	1	25
Munich, Germany	2	21
Copenhagen, Denmark	3	11
Berlin, Germany	4	16
Prague, Czech Republic	5	45
Haifa, Israel	6	101
Antwerp, Belgium	7	77
Zurich, Switzerland	8	14
Ottawa, Canada	9	30
Birmingham, United Kingdom	10	47
Seoul, South Korea	11	8
Geneva, Switzerland	12	9
Tallin, Estonia	13	54
Lyon, France	14	55
Liverpool, United Kingdom	15	48
Oslo, Norway	16	28

City, Country	Social Cohesion Ranking	CIMI 2015 Ranking
Kuwait, Kuwait	17	119
Basel, Switzerland	18	42
Manchester, United Kingdom	19	43
Bratislava, Slovakia	20	83
Melbourne, Australia	21	17
Linz, Austria	22	63
Leeds, United Kingdom	23	71
Nottingham, United Kingdom	24	75
Taipei, Taiwan	25	64
Florence, Italy	26	50
Osaka, Japan	27	56
Tel Aviv, Israel	28	97
Nagoya, Japan	29	87
Boston, United States	30	5
Dubai, United Arab Emirates	31	65
Stuttgart, Germany	32	51
Brussels, Belgium	33	32
Warsaw, Poland	34	74
Bursa, Turkey	35	128
Nice, France	36	61
Taichung, Taiwan	37	112
Doha, Qatar	38	117
Auckland, New Zealand	39	29
Amsterdam, Netherlands	40	6
Kaohsiung, Taiwan	41	103
Cologne, Germany	42	52
Vancouver, Canada	43	20
Lille, France	44	79
Ljubljana, Slovenia	45	86
Almaty, Kazakhstan	46	125

City, Country	Social Cohesion Ranking	CIMI 2015 Ranking
Vienna, Austria	47	26
Zagreb, Croatia	48	107
Hamburg, Germany	49	41
Rotterdam, Netherlands	50	70
Montreal, Canada	51	38
Valencia, Spain	52	49
Marseille, France	53	72
Riga, Latvia	54	78
Abu Dhabi, United Arab Emirates	55	66
Vilnius, Lithuania	56	89
Toronto, Canada	57	24
Glasgow, United Kingdom	58	46
Göteborg, Sweden	59	57
Stockholm, Sweden	60	27
Porto, Portugal	61	76
Frankfurt, Germany	62	35
Bilbao, Spain	63	69
Manama, Bahrein	64	138
Budapest, Hungary	65	68
Baltimore, United States	66	18
Seville, Spain	67	67
Buenos Aires, Argentina	68	85
Tokyo, Japan	69	12
Sydney, Australia	70	10
Lisbon, Portugal	71	62
Busan, South Korea	72	91
Medellin, Colombia	73	99
Sofia, Bulgaria	74	95
San Francisco, United States	75	4
Duisburg, Germany	76	73

City, Country	Social Cohesion Ranking	CIMI 2015 Ranking
Wrocław, Poland	77	94
Dallas, United States	78	19
Minsk, Belarus	79	137
Santiago, Chile	80	80
Houston, United States	81	31
Eindhoven, Netherlands	82	59
Riyadh, Saudi Arabia	83	123
Shenzhen, China	84	130
Montevideo, Uruguay	85	121
Naples, Italy	86	90
Monterrey, Mexico	87	102
Milan, Italy	88	44
Madrid, Spain	89	34
Jerusalem, Israel	90	105
Paris, France	91	3
Bangkok, Thailand	92	84
Porto Alegre, Brazil	93	118
Bangalore, India	94	176
Guangzhou, China	95	104
Washington, D.C., United States	96	13
Barcelona, Spain	97	33
Bucharest, Romania	98	110
Turin, Italy	99	82
Phoenix, United States	100	40
Manila, Philippines	101	145
Córdoba, Argentina	102	106
Chicago, United States	103	7
Saint Petersburg, Russia	104	133
Novosibirsk, Russia	105	154
Daegu, South Korea	106	98

City, Country	Social Cohesion Ranking	CIMI 2015 Ranking
Delhi, India	107	174
Guadalajara, Mexico	108	116
Tbilisi, Georgia	109	135
Philadelphia, United States	110	23
Tainan, Taiwan	111	141
Los Angeles, United States	112	15
Amman, Jordan	113	160
Miami, United States	114	53
Wuhan, China	115	153
Ankara, Turkey	116	127
Málaga, Spain	117	58
Curitiba, Brazil	118	129
Daejeon, South Korea	119	96
Tianjin, China	120	166
Istanbul, Turkey	121	109
Singapore, Singapore	122	22
Dublin, Ireland	123	36
Mexico City, Mexico	124	100
Brasília, Brazil	125	136
Tunis, Tunisia	126	144
Rosario, Argentina	127	134
A Coruña, Spain	128	60
London, United Kingdom	129	2
Kolkata, India	130	179
Hong Kong, China	131	39
Belo Horizonte, Brazil	132	152
Chongqing, China	133	147
Shenyang, China	134	155
Harbin, China	135	169
Suzhou, China	136	165
Shanghai, China	137	93

City, Country	Social Cohesion Ranking	CIMI 2015 Ranking
Kuala Lumpur, Malaysia	138	88
Beijing, China	139	92
Bombay, India	140	167
Recife, Brazil	141	142
Cali, Colombia	142	126
Lima, Peru	143	122
Cape Town, South Africa	144	120
London, Canada	145	37
Guayaquil, Ecuador	146	148
Bogotá, Colombia	147	111
Fortaleza, Brazil	148	149
Rome, Italy	149	81
Quito, Ecuador	150	132
Durban, South Africa	151	159
San José, Costa Rica	152	131
Jidda, Saudi Arabia	153	115
Baku, Azerbaijan	154	150
Moscow, Russia	155	108
Belgrade, Serbia	156	114
Kiev, Ukraine	157	143
Pretoria, South Africa	158	164
São Paulo, Brazil	159	124
Athens, Greece	160	113
New York City, United States	161	1
Skopje, Macedonia	162	146
La Paz, Bolivia	163	168
Santa Cruz, Bolivia	164	171
Salvador, Brazil	165	151
Guatemala City, Guatemala	166	161
Casablanca, Morocco	167	163

City, Country	Social Cohesion Ranking	CIMI 2015 Ranking
Jakarta, Indonesia	168	170
Johannesburg, South Africa	169	140
Caracas, Venezuela	170	162
Douala, Cameroon	171	175
Sarajevo, Bosnia and Herzegovina	172	157
Ho Chi Minh City, Vietnam	173	158
Karachi, Pakistan	174	181
Cairo, Egypt	175	156
Lagos, Nigeria	176	180
Alexandria, Egypt	177	173
Santo Domingo, Dominican Republic	178	172
Rio de Janeiro, Brazil	179	139
Nairobi, Kenya	180	178
Tehran, Iran	181	177

www.ingramcontent.com/pod-product-compliance
Lightning Source LLC
Chambersburg PA
CBHW070048210526
45170CB00012B/617